# GARDENING *from* SCRATCH

# Gardening from Scratch

ANN LOVEJOY

*Photographs by Allan Mandell*

*Illustrations by Jean Emmons*

Macmillan • USA

MACMILLAN
A Simon & Schuster Macmillan Company
1633 Broadway
New York, NY 10019



Manufactured in the United States of America
*Designed by Amy Trombat*

*ISBN 0-7394-0140-8*

FRONTISPIECE *Well-designed entry gates and walkways are an invitation to enter the garden. Narrow spaces like this one can be visually enlarged by layered plantings that mask nearby building walls.* GARDEN DESIGNED BY ERYL MORTON, VICTORIA, BRITISH COLUMBIA.

*For Kevin Nicolay and Elizabeth England,*
*beloved garden design mentors*
*whose influence lives on*
*though they are gone.*

# contents

**Introduction**
*ix*

ONE

**Begin at the Beginning**
*Where to Begin, What to Do First, and How to Do It*
*1*

TWO

**Exploring Your Options**
*Developing a Functional Garden Plan for Any Setting*
*17*

THREE

**Imagining the Garden**
*How to Design the Garden of Your Dreams*
*31*

FOUR

**Enclosure and Garden Rooms**
*Creating Places to Be in the Garden*
*47*

FIVE

**Getting Down to Earth**
*Big Projects Come First*
*79*

SIX

**Practical Paths**
*Simple, Handsome Paths to Make in a Weekend*
*93*

Seven

**Dirt Work**
*How's Your Dirt? Testing, Amending, and Building Your Soil*
*105*

Eight

**Mulches and Compost**
*Making Mulch and Compost–Feeding Plants and Combating Weeds*
*121*

Nine

**Building Better Beds and Battling Weeds**
*How to Create Optimal Planting Places within the Garden*
*137*

Garden Design Ideas

Design One

**Urban Condo**
*A Year-round Entry and Patio Garden in a Tiny Space*
*147*

Design Two

**Suburban Neighborhood**
*A Sunny Space for Flowers, Vegetables, Kids, and Pets*
*151*

Design Three

**Rural Retreat**
*Working with Shade, Combining Natives and Ornamental Garden Plants*
*155*

**Index**
*160*

# INTRODUCTION

THIS BOOK WAS BORN OF A WEEKLY COLUMN, also called *Gardening from Scratch,* which I write for my local island newspaper. The column, in turn, was my response to hundreds of questions I have received over the years from readers of my books and articles. Though they varied in detail, the main points were always similar. Where do I start? Even more basic than that, how do I figure out what I really want?

A bewildering number of practical handbooks direct the new gardener through the physical process of building a garden. Only rarely, however, are the philosophical questions that should underlie garden design even addressed. It is quite difficult to collect adequate information, much less use it effectively, when you aren't really sure what you are supposed to be doing.

*Gardens that reflect their setting as well as the sensibilities of their owners are endlessly satisfying havens for family and friends. (Garden designed by Pamela Burton, Santa Monica, California.)*

This book attempts to demystify the garden design process by explaining the principles that inform every stage, from fact gathering to the variety of practical applications which result in a satisfying garden. Designers who are fully aware of a site's essential elements and qualities can create a garden that not only reflects personal taste but displays a unique spirit of place.

It's important to make a garden that is practical, beautiful, and functional. It is equally important to make a garden that engages with its environment *and* architectural setting, in every sense. Most of all, we need to garden with an ecological awareness that acknowledges and plays upon regional differences.

This doesn't mean that we can't grow plants we love because they aren't native, or that we can't have a lawn if we really adore lawns. It does mean that as we move (as we are very apt to do), we must be flexible enough to grow with each garden. We can't keep making the kind of garden we loved in Philadelphia if we now live in Santa Fe. Each garden should be about you and about where you live.

I have been making gardens for most of my life, starting in Massachusetts and working my way west, with stops in Ohio, Colorado, and Montana before landing in gardeners' paradise here in the Pacific Northwest. Some of those gardens were lasting, others fleeting, but all were gardens of place, gardens that reflected both region and neighborhood.

Recently, life changes have contrived to make me build three brand new scratch gardens in as many years. Though all three are located within the space of just a few miles, each one is unique. This dissimilarity reflects changes in my taste; fluctuations in my time, energy, and budget; and the varying requirements of each setting.

Even more significant, however, were my assumptions and beliefs about what a garden should be. The depth of these surprised even me at first. For instance, I had fully intended to repeat certain beloved sections of my old farmhouse garden in my newest meadow garden. Instead, however, I became too excited about planting the new garden appropriately to remember to copy the old one.

In writing *Gardening from Scratch,* I offer you the practical and philosophical tools with which to make your own garden of personal delight. I hope you have as much fun in the process as I do. Indeed, I find garden-making becomes more joyful every time, as each new garden more closely approximates that inner garden hidden in the garden-maker's heart.

*Ann Lovejoy*

BAINBRIDGE ISLAND, WASHINGTON

ONE

# BEGIN AT THE BEGINNING

## Where to Begin, What to Do First, and How to Do It

*Making gardens from scratch is enormously exciting. Before anything has been done to turn that empty yard into a living garden, almost any option is possible. A brand new* garden is a blank canvas, ready to be painted with living pigments. The problem, of course, is figuring out what kind of garden pictures we want to see. When the possibilities seem endless, narrowing down those choices can be confusing. The most difficult part is deciding where and how to start. With absolutely everything to be done, where on earth do we begin?

*A welcoming path lined with clustered and generously planted pots entices us to wander further into the garden. The path is wide enough to make a living wall of pots that screens the open lawn from our eye while providing tantalizing glimpses of what lies beyond. (Garden of Lucy Hardiman, Portland, Oregon.)*

It is always best to begin at the beginning. The first step is to determine "where you are." Clearly, we all know where we live in the general sense, but in order to turn a yard into a garden, we need a lot of specific information about our place. You may already be aware of many of your property's quirks, qualities, and characteristics, but a surprising amount remains to be discovered in almost any location.

## MAPPING OUT YOUR LAND

The very first step on this journey of discovery involves making a map of the piece of land you plan to work with. If you are lucky, you may have a blueprint or surveyor map in hand. This can be enormously helpful, especially if the property has notable changes of grade or elevation, which are hard for amateurs to accurately measure. If you don't have such a map, don't despair, for a workable property map is quite easy to assemble, though it does take a bit of time.

If you do have a map, don't just copy it, but get out there and examine things for yourself. The point of this project is not only to find out all you can about the space in which you will be working, it is also a way of assessing and refining your own desires, dreams, and demands for the garden in the making. Use that ready-map as a reference point, certainly, but don't stop there. Take yourself outside and look around, taking time to really see what you have to work with. It's easy to develop general impressions that remain largely vague, even when we use or visit the area in question daily. Until we want to make something of the place, this general impression suffices nicely. When we want to make the most of our situation, however, it pays to give our genuine attention to each square foot of our yard, if only for a few minutes.

First impressions are often emotionally accurate, so don't overlook them. Take a sketchbook with you and jot down any general feelings each area inspires in you as well as more solid information. One corner of the yard may feel hushed and private, since it isn't overlooked by neighbors and street noise is blocked by the garage. The area under the kitchen windows may feel cheerful because it's sunny

and protected from wind, while the yard outside the master bedroom is dankly shady and a little depressing. Make notes, too, about how each area strikes you from inside the house.

In places where you are thinking about gardening from scratch, the windows aren't likely to be clogged with overgrown shrubs, but it can happen, especially in undeveloped yards where the only plantings are huddled around the house. If the views into the garden area are blocked, you will probably want to prune, if not remove the offending plants. They can often be repositioned elsewhere, providing a valuable air of maturity, so don't just run out there and cut them to the ground.

If the windows are not obstructed, think about how they might be framed with plants. A trellis arch or rectangular box frame can be set around a sunny window,

*The sunniest spots in the garden can be reserved for evergreen herbs and heat lovers which will appreciate the extra warmth of reflected light from nearby paving or hard surfaces. (Garden of Elizabeth England, Victoria, British Columbia.)*

making a deep recess that shades the room from excess western light. A climbing rose would embower that room in roses come summer, while Boston ivy (*Parthenocissus tricuspidata*) and a bird feeder would encourage a constant stream of lively company.

Make notes about what you presently see from each important window. Sometimes there will be splendid views, or at least not unattractive ones. In other cases, the view will be of things you would rather not overlook. We will look at view improvement in more detail later, but it's never too early to begin thinking about what you would like to see from each window when looking out into the garden.

*Doors and windows are good places to begin planning the garden's design. Thoughtful plantings can feature seasonal interest and include evergreen plants that frame garden views all year-round. (Garden of Roger Raiche, Berkeley, California.)*

### Starting a Working Map

When you begin transferring all this secondary information to your emerging map, the result very often looks cluttered or awkward. Lots of people panic at this point and either quit or send out frantically for help. Don't worry; everybody's initial attempts are less than perfect. French cooks always say the first pancake is for the dogs, and for most of us, the first map should be considered somewhat in this light. It helps to remember that you aren't in an art class. It's just a working map, and it's best made by you, not a hired professional.

The point is not so much 100 percent accuracy as for you and your yard to better your acquaintance. However rough artistically, a map made by you, based on your direct observations, will be of far more help in guiding the imaginative part of your garden-making than one made by anybody else. What matters here is not skill but knowledge and understanding of the existing conditions. The point is that you be able to make the garden you want, one that suits your needs and tastes and pleasures.

With perseverance, absolutely anyone can master the basic mapping techniques involved. People who consider themselves artistically challenged tend to judge their own efforts with exceptional harshness. Relax, loosen up your arm, and try again. Make several versions, varying drawing style or pencil softness, before tossing in the pencil and deciding you need help. Even if you absolutely don't draw, don't panic: Since our mapping mostly involves marking the corners with dots and connecting them with straight lines, graph paper and a ruler are great levelers. All degrees of experience and skill are equalized when connecting the dots.

Luckily, the first part of map-making is extremely simple. All you need to do is indicate the overall shape of your piece of land. Since most are more or less rectangular, the only tricky part is getting your sketch relatively proportionate. (If your property is an eccentric shape, it is just a little trickier: try to approximate, using the closest geometric shapes[md]usually triangles.) This is where the graph paper comes in; if your drawing skills are uncertain, that grid helps enormously, because you can decide that each square represents one foot or five feet or whatever size is convenient.

A long tape measure and a patient friend will be of great assistance during this phase. A twenty-five-foot tape will do, but if your property is of any size at all, it is worth splurging on a hundred-foot cloth tape. The best kind come on reels, with a pronged catch on the business end. This can be hooked over a tree branch or a windowsill if nobody is available to hold the end for you. These reel tapes are favored by builders for good reason. Since they cost under thirty dollars, it isn't a major investment, but it will ease your measuring struggles quite a bit.

If your property is very large, it is a good idea to map it in sections. The area around the house is generally best handled as one map, but if you have a long driveway or a deep backyard, those sections can be mapped and planned individually.

Once you have measured and marked the outlines of your property, you can record both key facts and those lingering impressions. Here is a checklist to help you discover what you need to

## YOUR PROPERTY CHECKLIST

HOW ARE THE HOUSE AND land oriented? First mark down the cardinal directions (north, south, and so forth). Now observe for a day or so how the sun moves across the property. Is the sun partially (or fully) blocked by neighboring houses or big trees? If so, when and for how long? Where will the sunlight fall in summer, when the sun is almost directly overhead? How about in winter, when the sun remains lower on the southern horizon? If you've spent a year in the house already, you may have a good idea about this. If not, you'll just have to make your best guess.

HOW WILL WIND AFFECT the garden? This is not only a concern at the beach or out on the prairie. In town, where houses or apartments are closely grouped, wind can tunnel through the gaps, creating destructive pathways that may damage plants in winter. Fencing, hedges, and even lightweight trellis can help deflect wind from seating areas and ornamental beds. Real trouble spots may make a great place for the compost heap and the garbage cans.

ARE THERE PLACES ALONG the house walls or under large trees where the ground stays dry even after hard rains? Are there places where rainwater puddles long after the rest of the yard is dry, or areas where persistent groundwater keeps the soil consistently moist? Map these, too.

WHAT KIND OF SOIL DO you have? Dig a few holes in several parts of the yard and see if and how it varies. Where I live, in the maritime Northwest, chances are excellent that the soil will be acid. East of the Cascade Mountains, where my parents live, it would almost certainly be alkaline. In your part of the world, the soil might be close to neutral in pH. Knowing your soil pH helps you select plants that will thrive for you.

Soil character can vary as well, for you might discover that you have sticky, heavy clay, or open, sandy soil, or some of each. In new developments, you may find almost impenetrable hardpan clay with a few token inches of cut-rate "topsoil" skimmed over it. Rarely will you be lucky enough to have neutral sandy loam, in which case you can grow just about anything you like with ease. (We will talk more about soil, how to know which kind(s) you have, and how to get it tested, in Chapter 7.)

HOW WILL THE YARD SPACE be used? Where does the dog sleep? (Is it where you want the dog to sleep?) Where will the kids play soccer? (Ditto.) Where will the meter man walk? (Remember, they all have huge feet.) Where will the garbage cans go? Which areas will you pass through frequently, and which rarely?

know about the place where you are living. Amend the list as you like, adding and subtracting questions to suit your circumstances.

This is just a partial list, but it gives you an idea of the kind of information you need to amass. As you do, that basic map will be expanding steadily. Over time, add details about things like weather and foot-traffic patterns

*The garden map offers us an overview of our property's overall shape. When we see the available space laid out clearly, we can imagine attractive and comfortable ways to use each area. Mapping also reveals traffic patterns and view lines that influence our garden design. (Garden of Roger Raiche, Berkeley, California.)*

as you learn them, or as they change. To facilitate all this input, keep a current copy of your basic map in your garden notebook so it can be updated periodically.

If you find yourself frequently changing and redrawing details while you are in this discovery stage, try covering your basic map with a clear acetate or plastic overlay. You can sketch on this with a waxy pencil and erase mistakes with a swipe of cloth before committing yourself to paper. This is also a good way to try out alternative design ideas. Sketch each plan onto a new overlay, and tape each onto the basic map by a single, different side (top, bottom, left, or right) to facilitate their interchangeable use.

The garden notebook or journal is as important and valuable a tool as the garden map. Fill it with everything that doesn't fit on your map, as well as with things that do—the overlap won't hurt anything, and it can help cement ideas in your memory. Organize them in any way you find most useful, whether by garden or map area, by topic, or even alphabetically. Three-ring binders are useful, since you can add pages when you accumulate more information on a topic than you expected to, but you can always tape extra pages into ordinary notebooks.

### Amplifying the Basic Map

However simple in execution, that basic map will have become the most useful guide you could possibly have by the time you are ready to begin the garden construction process. Making the map will be an ongoing project, developing continually over time as you learn more details about the land you live on. The second part is almost as

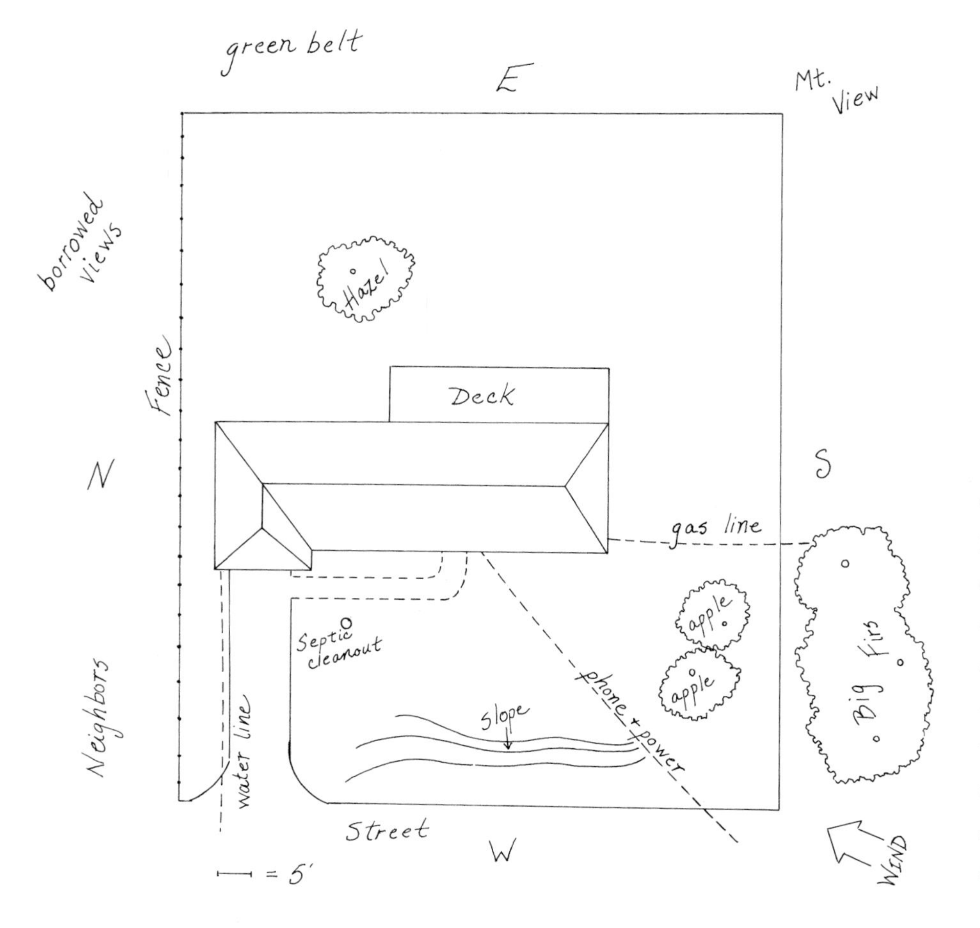


*The garden map will become your garden design guide, assisting you in project planning and plant placement and reminding you of all vital design factors at a glance. Don't worry if you lack drafting skills; simple bubble drawings are perfectly sufficient.*

simple as the first; once you have recorded the shape and size of the property, all you need to add is a reasonably accurate outline of the house and any other buildings, such as a garage, shed, or gazebo. It will be helpful later if their relative positions are accurate, but don't worry about it too much. When you need to design decks or paths or whatever for any given area, you can make another map just of that particular spot and work from that.

### Mapping Hardscapes and Grades

The third step is to add all existing hardscape to your map. This means anything man-made, from paths to patios. Record their present position, whether you intend to keep them or not. Walls of all sorts are also hardscape, both garden or boundary walls and those of the house or garage which might be included in the garden design. Fences, arbors, and trelliswork count too, as do steps, sidewalks, and driveways. Start by taking a careful inventory, then transfer them to the map. You don't need to draw or describe these things in great detail, but mark them in some way that helps you remember that part of the yard is already taken up with something structural.

It's amazingly easy to develop paper gardens that have increasingly little to do with the reality of your yard. "Oh, come now," you're probably thinking, "how could anybody forget a driveway or a huge tree?" The fact is, the drawing takes on a reality of its own. If the driveway or the tree isn't indicated, before you know it, its space has been taken over by a hypothetical herb garden. Not until you walk outside to start staking out the projected beds do you realize with chagrin that there is a slight technical problem.

Another point to consider is the lay of your land. Some yards are flat as a board, with grass that looks like a billiard table. This is great for the lawn mower, but less inviting for the gardener, who usually values changes of grade for adding visual interest to the garden. In such situations, you might want to explore making raised beds to give the garden more character. This doesn't always require the services of a bulldozer; one easy way to do this is to have good topsoil brought in and dumped right where you want to garden. Smooth it out, giving the mound a pleasing shape and tapering the soil so it drops in a natural-looking curve to meet the grass, and you have yourself an instant new bed.

The crown of your mound can be as high as you like, but the bed should be not less than twelve to eighteen inches deep overall. You may have to trim away the outermost foot or two of grass at the bed's edge, where the soil slopes to its shallowest depth. This is just insurance against rampant grass incursions into your new bed. Deeper into the bed, the weight of the mounded soil is enough to kill off the underlying grass without the bother of removal. On a larger scale, raised mounds called berms can be created (with the help of that bulldozer) which not only make

visually interesting shapes to plant but can also help screen the house and garden from passersby, overly close neighbors, or traffic noise.

Most yards, however, have one or more areas with varying grades. The ground may slope gradually, fall in graceful tiers, or the land may drop off abruptly. Garden designers show this change by shading and cross-hatching (making a series of short pencil marks in two directions). Topographic maps indicate elevation changes by outlining the shape of each level at given intervals. In big-scale maps, each line represents a change of ten or even a hundred feet. It's worth recording even tiny grade changes, especially in garden settings. Whether you want to emphasize or eliminate them, grade changes of even a few inches can cause problems or present possibilities.

*A steep hillside can be made more accessible by a wide, winding path which cuts in gentle switchbacks through the woods. Here, arches lead eye and foot along a path designed to facilitate access to the lower garden without removing any mature trees. (Garden designed by Michael Schultz, Sherwood, Oregon.)*

There are lots of ways to record them. Mapmakers use sets of concentric circles or blobs to indicate rising mounds of earth. A cliff would be marked with a series of closely spaced lines, rather like steps. It doesn't really matter what notation system you use, so long as you can remember what your symbols mean later on. Indeed, the point of all of this—both the observation and the map recording—is to assist your memory. When you begin dreaming about your garden, imagining what features could go where, the experience gained in mapping will

*Property with steep or significant changes of grade can be terraced to make hill climbing less strenuous. Here, decks and patios alternate with deep and richly planted beds and wide, stepped paths minimize the slope. (Garden designed by Dan Borroff, Tacoma, Washington.)*

help you retain a fairly accurate impression of the real situation out there: That large, blank expanse on your map might appear to be the perfect spot for the reflecting pool you always wanted, until you go back outside and realize that the area in question drops ten feet over a stretch of five yards. Whoops. Well, hey, how about a little streambed linking a couple of tiny ponds, with a recirculating pump to get the water back up that hill?

Where elevation changes are significant, as when a steep bank marks the front of the lot, sketch a side view to show how wide the bank is from top to bottom. This gives you a good idea about how much overall space is actually involved. That way, when the time comes for you

*Even small, urban gardens like this one may have a wonderful treeline (like a skyline, but alive). Borrowed views can include trees on neighboring or distant properties which contribute a comforting sense of green enclosure to the garden's ambience. (Lonesomeville, Portland, Oregon.)*

to start planting each area, you won't plan for or buy too few or too many plants to fill the bed.

### Making a Plant Inventory

Once your initial map of physical characteristics is made, you can start to figure out exactly what you have to work with. The next step in this process is to expand your map information by taking a detailed plant inventory.

Few yards are truly empty slates. Generally, there will be a tree or two (usually a maple and a flowering cherry) and a few shrubs (probably a lilac and a rose of Sharon), whether youthful or elderly. New houses are often fronted by large rivers of mulch, dotted here and there with juniper tams or dwarf spireas. Nearly always there is a lawn of some sort.

There may be "borrowed views" of plants. These can range from a splendid view of your neighbor's perennial borders to a magnificent old maple tree growing next door, or a healthy stand of conifers across the street. Unless the plants are dead or dying, it's best to simply record them before making a decision as to whether they have a place in your future garden.

When you record large trees, it's helpful to mark them with double rings, one to show the size and placement of the trunk, the other to indicate the spread of the canopy. Some trees may overhang the house or garage roofline, while others may intersect with each other. These situations can be indicated by making those parts of the ring lines dotted instead of unbroken. When you record them, estimate the height of any large plants as closely as you can, and evaluate their general shape and condition. Some shade trees, for instance, cast a gloom over the whole yard, yet are very beautiful. With selective removal or thinning of the lower limbs, the yard could receive far more light and air without sacrificing the graceful, natural lines of the tree.

Consider, too, what each tree contributes to the overall feeling of the garden. A badly butchered tree may lack any grace at all, yet be worth keeping, simply for its privacy or screening value, until a replacement has had time to grow up a bit. That thought is worth noting as well, for it's easy to be cavalier about clearing when "chain saw fever" strikes, but "oops" won't replace a tree mistakenly felled in haste.

As you make your garden inventory, walk the property and take notes about any horticultural assets you can identify. Add all of the plants you find to your list, including natives. Often undervalued, native plants can be your best bets in a new garden, especially if you are dealing with a difficult site or climate. Don't discount volunteer plants of any kind except outright thugs—things like stinging nettles or brambles. Think of natives simply as uncultivated trees, shrubs, perennials, and ground covers. You may have been considering all of them as weeds, as many

### TAKING STOCK

Before making any firm decisions about what's a keeper and what isn't, record the approximate size or age and overall condition of each plant on your map. I do it like this:

> One small vine maple, ten feet tall, looks healthy (definite keeper).
>
> One Norway maple, ten feet tall, looks healthy (probably remove—will get too big, is brittle, sheds branches, produces lots of yard litter).
>
> Six clumps of salal, three feet across, healthy (keep).
>
> Two sword ferns, huge clumps, will look great once cleaned up (keep).
>
> One pink rose bush, name unknown, rambling over wooden fence, has black spot on foliage, small flowers without much scent, lots of thorns, and gets powdery mildew in summer (remove).

folks do, but chances are excellent that these willing workers will grow well for you with very little assistance. Properly placed and cared for, native plants can be every bit as beautiful as garden center exotics, which are, after all, just somebody else's weeds from another part of the world.

If you don't know what sort of maple or other tree you have and wonder how it will grow later in life, help may be close at hand. A wonderful program administered through most county extension services is available all year for just such problems. To identify any plant you don't know, call the local Master Gardener program at the county extension service office. Ask when and where their next free public clinic will be held, then take samples of leaves, flowers, fruit, or whatever to be identified. (They also identify pests and diseases from samples of injured foliage.)

You can also take leaf samples to your local nursery, where identification assistance can generally be found as well. Indeed, if nobody there can help you, consider shopping around until you find a nursery where such help is available. Nursery cruising is great fun anyway, and you may discover all sorts of delightful plants (and people) during your search.

Once you have figured out which plants you have in your garden, you may well need to gather more information about them. An easy-to-use, regionally appropriate reference book will help enormously (see Chapter 9 for suggestions). However, garden books can be expensive, and not all are equally useful. To find out which will work for you, check several out of the library and try them out for a few weeks before buying anything.

As you discover plant names and gather interesting information about them, add all these things to your map and garden journal. Over time, an accurate, detailed portrait of your yard will emerge. As it does, your garden is growing and you are becoming a gardener.

TWO

# EXPLORING YOUR OPTIONS

## Developing a Functional Garden Plan for Any Setting

*Well-designed gardens combine practicality with lasting beauty. The very best gardens have an element of fantasy and visiting them is a transformational experience. This steep cliff is covered with evergreen shrubs arranged to make the tumble of water and huge rocks seem utterly natural. (Israelit Garden designed by Michael Schultz, Portland, Oregon.)*

*By the time you have fully explored your yard, you will have acquired a great deal of practical information about the place where you want to make a garden. Before you* begin the next, more active phase of the design process, take a good look at your garden map.

If you are like most people, your original clean sheet has become a tattered mess, covered with illegible scrawls. If it seems overly crowded already and you find it hard to read all your notes and observations, this would be a good time to redraw your map, expanding your original sketch to a more workable size. Before choosing one arbitrarily, ask your local copy shop about the largest paper sheet they can copy at a reasonable price. This matters, because soon that plan is going to multiply like happy bunnies.

If your drawing skills don't extend to enlarging the map yourself, get the copy shop folks to blow it

*Even small gardens can serve many needs if they are designed to take advantage of natural conditions. This small but sunny area holds raised beds for herbs and vegetables, an assortment of flowers, a graveled play area, and a hammock for relaxing. (Garden designed by Jeff Glander, Tacoma, Washington.)*

up for you. Keep going until you can read everything easily. Once you find the optimal size, copy your physical map at least a dozen times. Set aside one copy as your master sheet, so you can make more if you need to (you probably will).

Your expanded map now holds all the information you have gathered about your property. Now it's time to gather in whoever else will be involved in making or enjoying the garden. This may mean your family (kids and pets included, of course), your partner, or a few garden-minded friends who can help out with experience and vision. Settle everybody down around the table and get ready to play.

## BUBBLE DIAGRAMS

When garden designers want to explore options and possibilities, they use what is called a bubble diagram. This is pretty much what you might imagine from the name: You take your pencil and draw loose circles and blobs to delineate various conceptual gardens. For example, over here, in this flat, sunny area, I'd like to have a deck and a hot tub, with narrow shrub borders surrounding the deck. Blob #1. Let's put the vegetable garden behind the garage, by the compost bins. It's sunny back there too, so things will grow well, and I won't have to look at the empty beds all winter. Blob #2. I know I want my herbs near the kitchen door, so how about here under the sink window? Blob #3. This open area that's overlooked by the same window would make a great play space for the kids. Blob #4. If we put the dog run and kennel back by the potting shed, he wouldn't bother the neighbors or trample through the garden. Blob #5. See? You've already got the hang of it.

### FANTASY VS. REALITY

When you begin to compare your fantasies with the dreams of others who will be sharing your garden, you may notice that these may not always appear to be compatible. If you have planned a quiet country retreat and the kids are looking forward to a theme park with water slides, you will definitely need to do some negotiating. Happily, even a small garden can be designed flexibly enough to satisfy everybody. The ideal garden combines the practical with the magical, providing scope for the imagination but not attempting what can't be done. You could, for instance, create a tropical-looking jungle, complete with rushing waterfall, even in a very small space. You could not, however, include a roller coaster (unless your community's zoning regulations are markedly different than most). With a firm basis in reality, you can build a dream garden to live and work in, and enjoy.

## The Point of Paths

As you plan, keep in mind the many ways in which you use the yard already. Where do people usually congregate? How does foot traffic flow? It's usually a mistake to try to reroute firmly established paths, which tend to run directly between points of high use or interest, perhaps connecting the back door with the garage or the swing set. Unless the proposed alternative is soundly practical, feet have a way of forgetting and you'll often find people (including yourself) stepping over the new path in favor of the more direct old one, even if it's now supposed to be a planting bed.

Raised beds and clearly defined paths help to keep traffic where it is intended to go. However, visual clarity is not always enough to ensure compliance with your ideas. Unless frequently used paths are at least fairly direct, they quickly become an annoyance. Meaningless wiggles do not make for charm in paths or beds. This doesn't mean everything needs to be laid out with a ruler; softer, more natural lines can be equally soothing to the foot as to the eye. Remember, though, that in path design, the simple is nearly always more effective (and a lot easier to use) than the ornate.

### *Easy Access Paths*

It's also worth thinking about what you want from each path. Some will be access routes, plain and simple, intended to get your guests to the front door or your heavily filled wheelbarrow to the compost heap without incident. Paths that are used in the performance of daily or frequent chores should always be as direct as possible, as wide as practical, and surfaced with material that remains nonslippery when wet or icy, such as crushed rock or rough-finished cement.

Big, rugged granite stones make dramatic garden steps, especially when they connect the garden to the house. However, skid painfully down them even once on a frosty or rainy night and you'll wish you had opted for broad, level, and slightly textured concrete steps instead.

Similarly, those charming herringbone brick paths look delightful in the garden, but when slick with damp leaves or moss, they become treacherous underfoot. Reserve the bricks for

*Make several copies of your master map before adding secondary details. If the map gets too messy to read, try blowing it up to a larger size at the copy shop. It's also helpful to use clear plastic overlays for each project, drawing the details with a fine-tipped marker.*

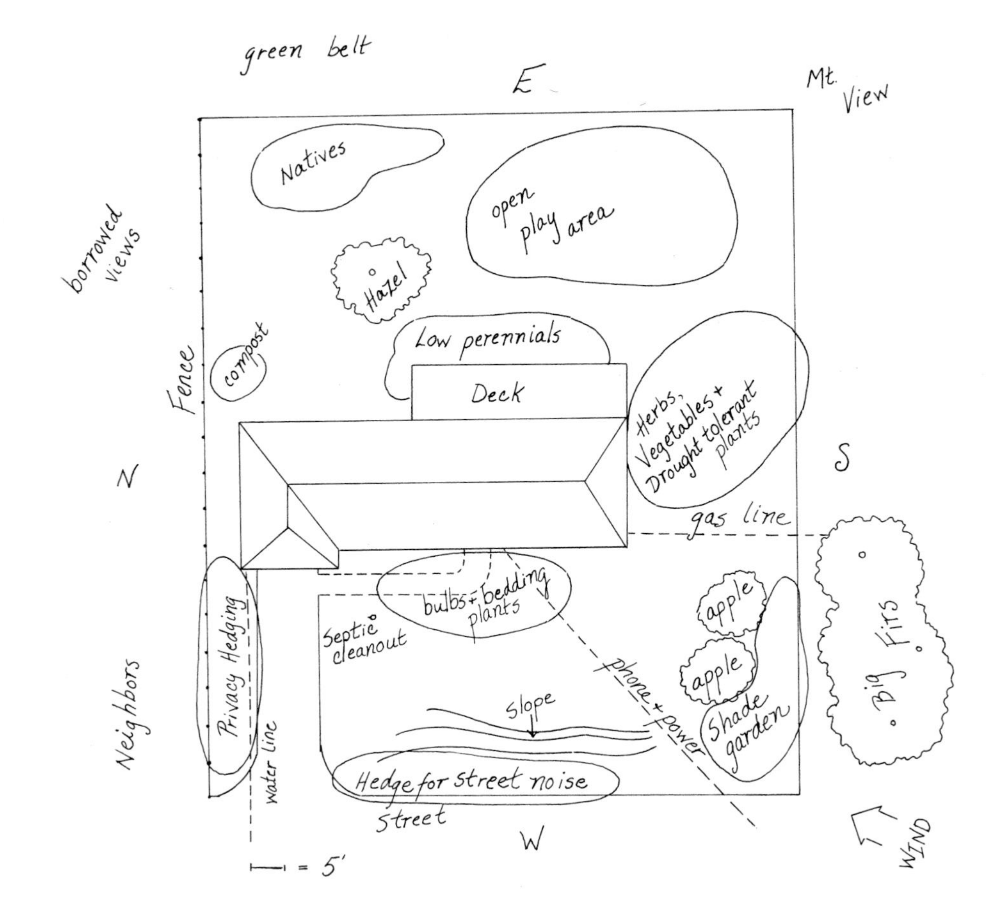

places you don't use often, or at night, and stick with safe, smooth surfaces for much-used paths and patios.

If grades must change significantly over the course of a major access path, keep the level changes bold and unfussy. If you need steps, as you probably will, make them broad and deep rather than narrow and abrupt. Think about what it might feel like to back down those steps in the dark with a ten-foot-long sofa on your head, and design accordingly. Think too about getting a baby and stroller up and down, and whether your aging grannie would require a handrail to negotiate those steps.

Even if you are young, agile, and single, it's useful to envision such possible scenarios. After all, your life could change any day, in dozens of possible ways. What's more, when potential buyers look at your house in the future, they might well have more complex needs. Taking a wide range of possible situations into consideration will encourage you to design a lastingly practical pathway flexible enough to meet many demands.

As you pencil in your probable path routes, consider not just the line of the path—whether it runs directly or wanders a bit—but also think about its overall size. Altering the shape and width of a path encourages us to use it in different ways. Straight paths lead us to our goals with no digressions. This is exactly what we want when rushing out to the garage to get to work or do carpool duty, or when moving heavy furniture into the house, but there are cases where directness is not an asset.

*Straight, wide paths work best for entering the garden and in any areas where there will be a lot of daily foot traffic. Large, lightly textured pavers without deep gaps help keep footing safe at night or in bad weather. Area lighting also contributes to nighttime safety. (Garden designed by Pamela Burton, Santa Monica, California.)*

*Entryway steps must be wide enough to allow for easy passage even when plantings spill over the sides. The treads must be deep enough to ensure safe footing at night or in bad weather. The boulders help to create slight terraces, breaking the fall of ground from the house to the sidewalk. This makes it easier to plant and disperses rain or hose runoff, leading excess water into planted areas where it can be absorbed. (Garden designed by Konrad Gauder, Vancouver, Washington.)*

### *Winding Paths for Gardens*

In the garden, arrow-straight paths march us briskly along, making us feel as if getting to the end of that path must be more important than noticing whatever happens to be occurring alongside it. Garden paths that meander encourage us to take our time about moving. Lazy curves recall slow streams lacing through sunny meadows. Paths whose twists and turns disguise their end point tempt us onward by offering glimpses of new plants or half-hidden seats. Such partial views make us feel that there is a lot to explore within even the smallest of gardens.

This holds true even in minute gardens where there is barely room for a path at all. Make that path straight, thinking to save space, and it will minimize the perceived size of the garden. Let it curve, loop, or double back on itself, and the garden seems far larger. Whatever we cannot read at a glance piques our curiosity and makes us wonder a bit. What's really out there? What comes next?

This sense of mystery is vital to a successful garden, for space that we take in all at a glance is almost never used. This is why open front yards are usually empty of life, while even partially enclosed backyards echo with the sounds of children and pets. People prefer to spend time where they feel both enclosure and welcome. Within the garden itself, partial views entice us to look further, while those that are laid out in one big swoop are less interesting to look at and less appealing to explore. Why bother? You can already see what's there. Well-designed paths turn full views into partial ones, drawing us inward and creating a series of intimate, interesting spaces instead of one large blank one. By directing our movement through the garden space in certain ways, paths can greatly alter the way we perceive that space.

While access paths need the strength of simplicity, paths that take us into and through the garden can be less purely utilitarian. Let these paths change in size, here narrowing as they pass through a slim arch or gate, now widening when we approach a lovely vista, whether inside the garden or beyond. When a path broadens to encompass a curve, that generous bulge creates a place to linger, so we can offer our attention to the plants around us. Wider spots become pools of quietness where we can drink in the growing greenness. A bench or solitary seat tucked into such a place draws use effortlessly.

*Entryways that are in constant use need clean, unfussy lines and uncluttered plantings. Pots can be positioned where they are constantly decorative yet never in the way. It's a good idea to allow plenty of access room for bringing in anything from groceries to baby strollers or furniture. (Garden designed by Pamela Burton, Santa Monica, California.)*

### Pleasing Places, Inviting Spaces

Architecture that acknowledges the way people naturally use or ignore space can help us make gardens where people feel welcome. Benches sited to psychological advantage are constantly popular, while those placed strictly for visual effect are seldom used. Given a choice, people all over the world choose seats that feel both secure and peaceful. Nearly always, this translates into

having something solid at our backs and an unfolding vista before our eyes.

In the garden, the preferred seats will be backed by a wall, hedge, or dense but rather plain plantings that lap slightly around the bench. From it, the sitter can see both the intimate details of the garden close at hand and a larger overview or vista beyond. This vista can be quite small and still be effective—anything that successfully leads the eye outward will work, whether a magnificent distant mountain, a small fountain close at hand, or a lovely plant in an ornamental pot. The combination of partial enclosure and extended view creates a cozy feeling of being embraced within the garden, without eliciting the claustrophobic reaction many people feel when small spaces, green or otherwise, have no apparent exit.

*Within the garden, curving paths create a pleasing sense of mystery. Small gardens can seem limitless when wandering paths and careful planting disguise the actual perimeters of the property. Trees and shrubs on neighboring land can be incorporated into the illusion, making an implicit extension of space. (Garden of Bobbie Garthwaite and Joe Sullivan, Bainbridge Island, Washington.)*

In practical terms, all these ideas have direct applications for garden makers. For instance, you may want to preserve a lovely stretch of open lawn to create views from smaller areas. Adding a specimen tree or two will break up its monotony and create a pocket of interest that can be further enhanced with small shrubs or simple mixed plantings. It quickly becomes obvious that awkward spaces like the narrow run between the garage and the house or that oddly shaped side yard will tend not to be used much or at all. However, when both a degree of enclosure (as from an archway, a gate, or a trellis) is introduced and an outward view (perhaps of the garden, or a lovely tree) is framed, such places can gain enough character and presence to become favorite retreats. Try experimenting with a few trellis panels and potted plants to see where this might work on your site, then sketch your ideas onto your map.

*Seats that are backed by solid-looking greenery but offer extended views prove more inviting than those perched in more open surroundings. People are also drawn to sunny seats in shady gardens, and shaded seats in sunny ones. (Garden of Cyril Hume, Victoria, British Columbia.)*

## Above and Below

By this point in the process, the impatient are anxiously fiddling with their pencils, wondering when they can trade them in for shovels. When do we get to the really exciting part, the situating of our plants? It is very tempting to skip these slower stages, rushing out instead to buy all the plants you want and putting them wherever seems good. This is, after all, a tried and true way to make a garden. Indeed, many quite charming little gardens have been started this way (some of them by me). However, if you have made haphazard gardens before and want more than accidental successes this time, or hope to avoid those unforeseen pitfalls that can waste such an astonishing amount of time and effort, not to mention money, be prepared to put up with a few more mechanics.

Buying plants before you have a workable plan is rather like choosing paint for walls of a house that isn't built yet. There's nothing wrong with that—indeed, it's a hopeful act, an expression of faith. In practical terms, though, there is a big difference; you can store paint in the garage for months, but potted plants need constant care. It's far less stressful to put off plant purchases until you have at least a nursery bed in place, concentrating instead on getting the big picture parts of the garden in place.

Before we leap into the delightful fray of active garden making, therefore, a few last details need addressing. Some of these don't matter much so long as your back and shovel are the most powerful tools you need for your garden-making process. However, these particulars become a lot more important if you are considering any changes to the property that will require the use of heavy machinery. Alterations in grade, major additions of topsoil, the removal or addition of large trees, pond excavation, and so forth all demand serious equipment.

Before the trucks and bulldozers arrive, be sure that you know a few key facts. Where, for instance, do the water and sewer lines run? Have you a septic tank? Where, exactly, is it? Many older homes may not have tanks at all, with sewage running out into a nearby meadow (or the garden). In other cases, the tank location has been long forgotten. Big trucks can often find out for you, generally by running over the hidden tank or feed lines, but it's more fun and far less messy to know such things ahead of time.

It is also a good idea to make a note on the map about where any power lines come in, especially those that are buried. Check out the television and cable hookup, too; in a newer house, even if you don't use it, that hookup is probably out there somewhere, just waiting to be accidentally cut.

Telephone lines, whether running high above ground or buried below, should also be marked on the map. That way, you won't forget and site a hopeful young tree where its mature life will be one of constant strife. No tree looks

*Well-chosen and well-placed trees never outgrow their position and remain a lastingly beautiful addition to the garden. There are hundreds of small trees like this starry magnolia that can live long and useful lives in gardens where larger trees would become unsuitable in time. (Garden of Bobbie Garthwaite and Joe Sullivan, Bainbridge Island, Washington.)*

its best when large sections of it are periodically whacked to shreds by the power company or telephone road crews. You'll save a great deal of trouble for everyone, including the tree, by simply not planting anything beneath power lines that will outgrow its position, either in your lifetime or that of future generations.

### Putting Trees in Their Place

Sadly, appropriate tree placement is a neglected art. Here in the Northwest, our backdrop is often majestic, featuring towering Douglas firs and huge hemlocks. Similar situations are common all across the country, from the great North Woods to the pine groves of the deep South.

Big garden trees do help tie the garden visually to such grand backdrops, but even if your yard is unusually large, there will probably be room for only one or two of the largest trees, those that top out between 60 and 100 feet. In most cases, it's far better for all concerned to select trees that will top out between 30 and 40 feet. This is an excellent time to think of the future, considering how each candidate tree might affect not just your own yard and house but your neighbor's property as well, before making your final choice.

I must reiterate: Before planting your tree—indeed, before planting anything that will get larger than you are—be very sure that it will never encounter anything it shouldn't either on the way up or down. This means being aware of overhead wires as well as underground pipes and whatnot. Anybody who has ever had a poplar or a willow tree infiltrate water or sewer lines doesn't need to hear this twice. However, if it hasn't happened to you yet, a word of warning may spare you from developing a closer acquaintance than you really want with the RotoRooter guy.

THREE

# IMAGINING THE GARDEN

## How to Design the Garden of Your Dreams

*When beginning a garden plan, it is smart to consider how you would like each area to look in winter. Benches, paths, walls, and fences combine with evergreen shrubs and trees to make up the garden "bones," the structural elements that hold seasonal plantings in place. (Garden designed by Jeff Glander, Tacoma, Washington.)*

*By now, those blobs and bubbles have made your garden map look fuller than ever. It's a good idea to wander back and forth between the yard and the drawing table during* this process, reminding yourself of details that flat paper can't convey. It's remarkable how much there is to record about what initially appeared to be an "empty" yard. Even though an enlarged map offers more room for writing, some information is too complex or lengthy to fit efficiently on it. Amplifying the map with a loose-leaf binder or notebook will help keep all those notes and observations organized.

Even if the yard or garden space is tiny, allow a whole notebook section for each area which is to have a distinct use or character. It may seem silly to do this at first when there's nothing much there, but as those specific details mount up, you'll have a lot to record and think about for every section. As entry, side yard, patio, driveway, and so forth reveal their particular qualities, you can develop increasingly specific design ideas, planting plans, and maintenance schedules for each.

All this documentation of physical objects and qualities will be of enormous help along the way, but another vital part of the garden-making process remains to be explored. The map reflects the realities of the garden and your ideas about what you want to see out there, but what about your dreams? Now it's time to start stretching the imagination, trying to see past what is to what could be.

The first question to ask is the most difficult: What do you want? That often stumps us for a while, because too many options are almost worse than too few. If anything is possible, how do you choose? It's helpful to begin with a visualization/dream session. Relax, there's nothing New Age about this; it's all part of the creative process. Just close your eyes and let garden pictures float through your mind. At first they may be vague and cloudy, but a few directive questions can sharpen the focus of your imagination.

What do you think about or see in your mind when you think about gardens? What is the overall feeling? Are you relaxed or stimulated? Is that inner garden sunny and bright with flowers? Are there formal knot gardens of herbs, billowy borders in ranked rows, or tumbling cottage beds? Perhaps instead you envision a cool, shady garden rich with ferns and mosses amid leafy shrubs and towering trees.

Now explore your imaginary garden in terms of other qualities. Consider noises, scents, and textures as well as colors. Do you hear bird song, humming bees, splashing

water, laughing children? Do you smell romantic roses and mock orange, brisk herbs, or sultry lilies and heady jasmine? Are the borders thick with bloom or interwoven with foliage in various forms and sizes? Are those bright beds solidly packed or threaded with airy grasses and spangled with small, open-textured shrubs? Do you envision muted pastels, joyful runs of jewel tones, or themed borders in two or three colors?

This imaginative exercise may present you with an interesting dilemma, as when you find that your inner garden is sunny and your present home is in full shade. The solution may lie in selective thinning of branches to allow

*Shade lovers can be gathered into cool glades beneath tall, embracing trees. In such spots, creamy or golden foliage gleams like sunlight. (Garden of Dan Heims, Portland, Oregon.)*

more light to certain areas. Where will you want to sit in summer? Would you prefer the sun in front, where others can enjoy the flowers too, or in back of the house, where you can sunbathe in privacy? At least one sunny area can be arranged for almost any situation.

Things are much easier when you long for shade and your garden site offers only unrelieved full sun. Young trees take time to grow, but buying one or two large ones would make a worthy investment, adding an immediate impression of maturity to the new garden. If the cost (which can range from a few hundred to many thousands of dollars) seems prohibitive, consider the many shade-producing alternatives.

Arbors create instant shade, especially if covered in lath as well as young plants. Plant whatever you intend to serve for long-term coverage, then embellish a bit with instant greenery. Stud the support posts with flat-sided hanging baskets full of tumbling annuals, position baskets of annual vines along the overhead beams, and your new arbor garden can rival old Babylon in no time. To make the best of it, plant for the future and build for the present.

*Sunny, open gardens allow us to grow a delightful array of flowers, but a shady seating area will be very welcome in summer. If the garden lacks mature trees, arbors and pergolas can be draped with vines and climbers to provide cooling shade for plants and people. (Garden of Lord and Lady Chatfield, designed by Cyril Hume, Victoria, British Columbia.)*

## PLANTING FOR PRIVACY

The concept of privacy will prove helpful at every step of the design process and often is a primary consideration in garden design. One of the most attractive and practical ways to achieve privacy is to enclose at least part of the garden with plants, either in a hedge or in hedgerows of mixed shrubs and small trees.

Hedge plantings give the resulting inner area a strong sense of place, turning wide open spaces into garden rooms which can then be given character and purpose to suit your needs. The living green walls block street noise and dust, temper winds, screen out unwanted views, and provide visual support for the decorative plants that fill the beds and borders.

The problem, of course, is that hedges take time to grow. If your budget is big enough, you can buy enough mature plants to accomplish all these purposes almost immediately. However, most of us have to work with significant budgetary restrictions. This may mean that large projects must be staggered over several years, and usually means that we will be working with relatively young and small plants rather than expensive, mature specimens.

*Ruffled, multilayered perimeter plantings of trees and shrubs link the garden to its greater setting, providing enclosure and visual privacy while preserving a relaxed, naturalistic feeling. (Garden of Ernie and Marietta O'Byrne, Eugene, Oregon.)*

In such cases, it proves most practical to arrange a cheaper, temporary means of enclosure until your baby hedge plants come of age. Fortunately, there are lots of ways to do this, as inventive gardeners all over the country have demonstrated.

One of my favorite small gardens is partially enclosed by large shrubs that form a dense backdrop for the curving beds. Where large gaps existed in the hedge, new young plants have been set in place, backed up by a line of elderly but still distinguished-looking wooden shutters over six feet tall. These were salvaged from the dump, but similar finds can often be had for the asking when old houses are slated for demolition.

Interestingly aged doors can also be used to make a surprisingly attractive temporary fence. Several urban gardeners I know have supplemented their sagging old fences with sturdier sections gleaned at an urban recycling center. What keeps such adaptations pleasingly funky

*Temporary enclosure can be created by all sorts of means, from trellis to fencing. These huge old shutters successfully screen this small garden from the road while young shrubs planted to block the view are growing up. (Garden of Lindsay Smith, Bainbridge Island, Washington.)*

instead of offendingly junky is the garden maker's strong sense of style. Those who can successfully pull off similar effects with vintage pieces in the house or with clothing can usually make it work in the garden as well.

If funk is not your thing, consider making an instant enclosure with inexpensive panels of prefabricated trellis. For a more solid backdrop, use soft fences of woven bamboo or reed grass. Hung from stout posts or woven into wire fences with twist ties, these natural fiber fences last a surprisingly long time. (One of mine still looked good after ten years, despite the battering effects of the weather.)

Where ugly but functional fences are in place, you can plant your young hedge about three to five feet in front of them, allowing for future growth. Next, figure out an appropriate and attractive remedial treatment for the fence. An old wooden fence near my house is painted with a wandering line of blue waves, each capped with a green fish. Another has been casually painted in a broken rainbow of muted colors. Rusted old barbed-wire fences can be made less objectionable by weaving them through with leggy fruit tree prunings to create a nicely textured wattle backdrop for the borders. Plain chain-link fences may be threaded with slim strips of cedar, either vertically or on long diagonals. Add a few climbing vines and you will soon have an effective visual barrier at very little cost.

### Screening Views

Another major point to consider is how you will see the garden from the house, and what you will see of the garden from various indoor rooms. Your map already shows the outline of the house,

*Fencing can be decorative or even sculptural in its own right, setting off view-screening plantings like a gallery wall. Where large plants will quickly create enclosure, short-term fencing can be made from inexpensive materials such as split bamboo or woven reed screens strung on wires. (Garden of Roger Raiche, Berkeley, California.)*

but now you can clearly indicate important windows and think about what you would like to be looking at from each of them. To do this, sit in front of each window and dream into its current view, imagining what could be out there.

Next, go out into the garden, making specific notes about conditions in each view spot. Make these notes as exact as possible, specifying shade and sun patterns, soil situations, and so forth. This way, you can go to a nursery armed with extensive information and get very accurate suggestions in return. It's a good idea to ask local nursery folks for plant recommendations, because they (presumably) know local conditions very well. However, the more practical information you can offer, both about the planting site and the characteristics of the plant you want, the more likely you are to get useful information.

If you can say, for instance, that you are looking for a good-size evergreen shrub that will mature at about eight or ten feet, spreading to perhaps half that in width, with a noninvasive

*The backyard of this urban property is enclosed with a combination of fencing and naturalistically layered hedging, creating an inner garden that is a quiet but colorful retreat. (Garden of Lucy Hardiman, Portland, Oregon.)*

root system, with a foliage color that will look bright in the shade, your chances of making a successful match between plant and ideal are vastly improved. When all you can ask for is "Something that will look nice in a dark corner," the odds are dramatically less in your favor.

As we have seen, outlooks from and views within the garden are also important. To identify the best potential places to admire existing views, take a chair out to the garden and spend a few minutes scouting in each likely spot. If there is (or you want there to be) a deck, patio, or seating area, observe what you can see from there as well.

If you are lucky, there will be at least something to be excited about. In this gorgeous country, beautiful views abound in every region. Magnificent trees, attractive houses, or neighboring gardens can all be adapted freely, as can views of woods, water, or mountains. Even the glitter of the cityscape can be beautiful (especially when softened by distance).

Unfortunately, such wonders may be all but obliterated by a large (and usually homely) building right next door. Both town dwellers and suburbanites may face significant visual challenges in developing potential views. Country folk may not have much problem with big condo units next door, but a surprising amount of visual clutter mars rural areas as well, from blue tarps on the woodpile to aging double-wide trailers parked smack in the middle of an otherwise scenic meadow.

In any situation, an imaginative approach will help us to make the best of what we have to work with. To do so, note any unattractive views that will need screening as well as the lovely ones. Any view can be downplayed or emphasized by careful framing with plants, trellising, or fencing.

How you screen views depends on where and what they are. Are neighboring houses so close that your yard is overlooked? Is the street loud with cars, the sidewalk busy with passersby? Covenants and local regulations often limit the height of fencing, but openwork trellis panels can sometimes be added to existing fences. Threading fence and trellis alike with climbing plants provides more privacy and muffles street sounds as well. Where space permits, evergreen hedges make even more effective barriers. As we have noted, hedges take time to establish, but it's worth the wait. Coupled with a fence for instant

*In suburban situations, neighboring houses may share a common hedge line and mature trees may be few. Quick-growing hedge plants that remain moderate in height at maturity (like these arborvitae, Thuja occidentalis 'Smaragd' or Chamaecyparis lawsoniana 'Ellwoodii') prevent future squabbles about covenant-preserved views. (Garden of Elaine and Dave Whitehead, Saanich, British Columbia.)*

*In tiny urban gardens there may be no dramatic views to capture, or wonderful mature plants to frame. The solution is to create inner views or miniature vignettes which remain attractive in any season. (Garden of Elaine and Dave Whitehead, Saanich, British Columbia.)*

visual privacy, even a young hedge soaks up an amazing amount of road noise.

Creative problem solving can transform ordinary spaces into genuinely delightful places to be. If neighborhood or street noise is annoying despite a fence, a small recirculating fountain can mask the disruptive sounds. If neighbors' dogs trek through the yard, even a low fence will change their travel plans. Drape it on your side with evergreen clematis and honeysuckle and enjoy the added benefit of less dust and noise.

When noting any kind of potential problems on your map, start thinking about possible solutions as well. Maybe you have a blocked, partial view of something splendid. Could you admire that sliver of Mount Rainier better if your eye weren't distracted by your neighbor's laundry line or their kids' swing set? You can't (usually) change the neighbor's yard, but you can certainly modify your own. If your kids' swing set or your dog's pen occupies the area with the best view, find another spot to move the obstruction. The whole family will benefit more if that lovely little view is preserved and framed instead of squandered on the dog or children too short to even notice it.

This is not callous, merely practical. Though the needs of all family members are valid, the garden will be a haven for everyone. A wonderful outlook, however small, lends an important sense of expansion to even tiny spaces. To give that scrap of view more importance, flank it with a pair of tall, narrow shrubs such as 'Skyrocket' junipers. Their upright lines will provide an instant frame for your picture. Next to them, plant a fast-growing evergreen like *Escallonia rubra* to block off the flapping laundry. Voilá! Now you see the mountain, not the molehills. (For more detailed information on how to frame beautiful views, please refer to Chapter 4, pages 74–77.)

*Making Your Own Views*

What if there is no mountain to see? Well, that's where the creative impulse comes into play. No matter how small the garden or how close the neighbors, there are plenty of ways to create little views and even vistas within the available space. When the possibility of expanding views outward are limited or nonexistent, we need to turn inward instead. Start thinking in terms of decorative elements or arrangements that are strong enough to satisfy the eye over a long period of time.

To make your own views, you once again begin by imagining what you might like to see. In some cases, delightful scenes can be painted on blank walls. This works best when the walls in question belong to you, or you have cooperative (or oblivious) neighbors. If painting a whole wall proves impractical, something considerably smaller may work just as well. In Regency England, gardeners built little stages with marvelously painted backdrops where they displayed their precious alpine primroses. One garden I know is backed by an unsightly old garage. To disguise it, the owner has draped the operative side with canvas painted like a stage set with blue sky and puffy clouds. If you aren't a painter yourself, hire a friend (or a starving art student) to paint you a favorite image, whether a soothing meadow, dramatic distant mountains, or the rolling sea.

You might prefer to employ a French-inspired painting technique called *trompe l'oeil,* which means "trick of the eye." The illusion of reality is created through the use of photorealistic imagery or false perspectives that imply distance, creating a visual extension of the actual space. *Trompe l'oeil* can also be worked with trellis panels, which are cut and refitted to suggest a similar false perspective, often mimicking a tunnel or archway which extends "through" a perfectly flat wall.

Another way to expand narrow gardens conceptually is by installing a handsomely weathered door in your wall, fence, or hedge. The door doesn't even need to open, for its mere presence implicitly amplifies the garden's size. Old window frames and sashes can work similar magic. Back them with a beautiful poster of the Swiss Alps, a photograph of a large garden, or a painted view of anything that pleases you. You can also replace or back their glass panes with a mirror to enlarge the garden through reflection. In every case, an abundantly planted window box hung below the sash will complete the illusion perfectly.

Larger garden mirrors will increase the garden's apparent size remarkably effectively. Mount them on walls or fences, or set them between the partially screening foliage of plants. In cramped courtyards or tiny patios, you can arrange a cluster of large potted plants to frame the mirror, whose edges will them be disguised. When possible, fasten the mirror securely to the nearest wall or fence to prevent breakage. If big mirrors are set among garden plants growing in the ground, take care to position them where they won't be blown down or knocked about by roaming pets at night. Either way, both the nearby plants and the more distant parts of the garden will be reflected in such mirrors, making a confined space feel more open.

Because mirrors reflect light as well as leaves, they brighten dark places outside just as they do indoors. Tiny, dim corners can be transformed by adding a hanging wall mirror and a few attractive containers filled with tough, shade-loving plants like Swiss mountain pine (*Pinus mugo*; zone 2, 8–30 feet tall), glossy, big-leaved *Fatsia japonica* (zone 7, 6–15 feet tall), or golden Lawson cypress (*Chamaecyparis lawsoniana* 'Lutea'; zone 5, 10–30 feet tall). Like many large shrubs and small trees, these adapt well to life in big containers, growing more slowly than they would in the ground.

**WATERSCAPES** Small water features make excellent focal points for interior garden views. Recirculating fountains can be hung on the walls of the narrowest passageways, turning them into echo chambers filled with ever-changing water song. We can choose among hundreds of free-standing fountains which take up only inches of space. Zenlike arrangements of natural rocks can be piped to exchange slim threads of running water. Shapely planting pots can be stoppered with marine plugs to make them watertight, then fitted with water bubblers or fountain heads. In one garden I know, an old spigot pours water continuously into a pretty watering can.

A little green-hedged space can be centered with a tiny reflecting pool, perhaps planted with a single clump of variegated water iris or a miniature water lily. A broad water basin can sit on a low table or pedestal, or merge with billowing plants at the edge of a flower bed, where it will attract bathing birds. The simplest water jar, placed near a bench, will reflect sun and stars and passing clouds upon its smooth surface. (An important footnote: Most free-standing water features will need to be drained or even brought indoors in winter, when freezing could damage them.)

*Water features make splendid focal points for small gardens which lack striking views. Inexpensive submersible pumps can turn a plain water jar into a small fountain or recycle a cheerful cascade like this one. (Garden of Robin Hopper and Judi Dyelle, Metchosin, British Columbia.)*

*Stone sculpture like this dreaming garden guardian carved by Marcia Donahue of Berkeley, California, remains compelling in any season. When supportively interplanted, garden art retreats to a secondary position in summer but emerges to full, gleaming glory in winter. (Israelit garden, designed by Michael Schultz, Portland, Oregon.)*

GARDEN ART Weatherproof sculpture of various kinds will comfort the eye when the garden is bare and mingle effectively with our plants when they are in leaf. Classic or sleekly modern pieces can work equally well, so long as they are properly placed. Generally, this means matching the strength or delicacy of the work with that of the surrounding planting. An intricate piece of art will be lost amid a fussy flurry of foliage, but will be seen to advantage against a clipped hedge or set between shrubs with strong lines and a simple texture.

Less complex pieces work almost anywhere. A minimalist piece such as a plain stone sphere both gains and adds strength when set within a planting of utter simplicity. Tossing waves of silky hair grass (*Deschampsia flexuosa*) or *Stipa tenuissima* can look a bit boring en masse, but the addition of that stone (or concrete or reflective glass ball) provides just enough contrast to make both the plants and the object seem far more interesting. Even a wide expanse of an ordinary ground cover like pachysandra or ivy will be transformed into a green art gallery when an appropriate object is introduced into its midst.

Often snubbed as mere decorations, such embellishments as these gain architectural importance in very small spaces. There, they function not just as ornaments but as potent focal points for interior views which make the garden seem less constricted. A playful approach to the common design problems caused by lack of space may encompass all these expansive tricks: mirrors and water, sculpture and painting. Keep them in mind when considering the possibilities offered by your developing garden, and potential problems may begin to seem like invitations to try a more adventurous design approach.

FOUR

# ENCLOSURE AND GARDEN ROOMS

## Creating Places to Be in the Garden

*Though most of us think about gardening in terms of plants, a big part of garden-making involves creating places to spend time out of doors. When we look past the accepted norms of* our own culture, we find that there are a lot of ways to go about this. The mosaic-tiled rose gardens of Persian Isfahan and the austere Japanese Zen temple gardens represent vastly different styles, as do the enclosed patios of Spain, formal French *allées*, and majestic Italian water gardens. However, to have general relevance for garden makers in North America, a garden style needs to be flexible. Very flexible.

*Wide open spaces are rarely inviting, but sheltered, cozy areas invite active use. Wrapping the garden in an embrace of plants softens the line of enclosing walls or fences, making the garden feel embowered rather than shut in. (Garden designed by Jeff Glander, Tacoma, Washington.)*

Consider, for instance, the needs of an average family of four. They will need a place for the kids to play soccer without hurting Mom's flowers or Dad's vegetables. The dog needs a pen and a run, and we also have to fit in a sandbox, a barbecue pit, and a seating area. Now, all these things can certainly be jumbled together, but a serene, harmonic effect is rarely created that way.

When we separate needs by category, we can allot each kind of activity its own space. If we then create divisions between the areas, each space takes on its own character and style. When you are sitting outside drinking your morning coffee, you can be looking at the flower beds instead of the laundry line or the swing set. When the children are sweetly playing outside, as children do, you have the option of *not* watching too closely.

Once you choose where you want these various activities to take place, you can decide whether to create visual baffles or physical boundaries between them. Unsightly areas should be completely screened off and, if possible, hidden away at the perimeters of the property. More attractive areas—in terms of both activities and visual interest—can be clustered nearer to the house. Places where you spend the most time can be made to overlap visually by using low interior divisions, or they can be partially or fully enclosed to encourage greater privacy and diversity.

It's a lot like being able to shut the door to your kid's room so you can enjoy the serenity of the living room undisturbed by visual clutter. The inner divisions of the garden can be made flexibly, so that they are easy to alter as your family's needs change. When your children are small, you may want to overlook their play yard at all times. As they become more independent, you both may want more privacy. Their outdoor room may start out full of climbing toys and end up empty as a ballfield. The beds

*Intimate, cozy garden rooms become inviting extensions of the house. Framed by pots or plantings, fences or walls, these outdoor spaces have the same sense of place that a house room offers. (Garden designed by John Pruden, Portland International Gardens, Portland, Oregon.)*

and borders in yours may be filled with protective barriers when children (and pets) are small, then open out to include reflecting pools and more complex plantings as everybody matures.

The idea of making garden rooms—different areas that have specific uses and styles—is both ancient and relatively new. Earlier in this century, an American expatriate, Lawrence Johnston, was living in England. There, he made a delightful garden called Hidcote, where a variety of garden rooms were developed. Near the house, they are fairly formal in flavor. As they get nearer the woods and meadows, the rooms become more romantic or naturalistic in planting.

In the warmer parts of the world, people have been doing a good share of living in their gardens since ancient times. Here in America, the concept didn't really catch on until the 1950s.

*Since the 1950s, outdoor living has become increasingly popular. Simple or fancy, garden structures such as gazebos, summer houses, and teahouses encourage us to eat and read and play in our gardens in any weather or season. (Garden of Shelly Johansson, Bainbridge Island, Washington.)*

These days, we take a lot of this for granted. Our parents' generation thought twice before altering standard plants and patterns for house foundation plantings or even ornamental beds. The idea of actually *using* the front yard would have been faintly shocking. A big, immaculately groomed front lawn was a status symbol, indicating a comfortable income. Who would risk planting anything else? These days, however, almost anything goes. Urban gardens may hold tiny orchards, and wildflower meadows may replace the sacred lawn in the heart of the suburbs.

The outdoor living movement got started after the war, beginning mainly in California. Thomas Church, a landscape architect who wrote a famous book called *Gardens Are for People* (Reinhold Publishing Company, 1955), stressed the importance of having places to entertain within our own gardens. Private swimming pools, decks, and patios sprang up everywhere, transforming the American backyard almost overnight.

## MAKING GARDEN ROOMS

If the idea of garden rooms appeals to you, this is the time to figure out where you want them. Garden rooms are best described as fully or partially enclosed areas within the yard. They vary in character, but are united in purpose as welcoming destination spots within the garden. Such places can sometimes be contrived with very little effort, which means they can be assigned to a later time slot on your garden design implementation schedule. Most, however, will require the addition of fencing, hedging, or trelliswork that is best put in place before the garden beds are planted.

Garden rooms can be as simple as a courtyard built between the house and the garage, using a wall from each building for the two longest sides and adding arched trellis panels or a pair of flanking evergreen shrubs to partially enclose the short ends. A garden entry room might consist of a walkway which runs from garden gate to the front door, bordered on both sides with entwined fruit trees or clipped privet. If the enclosed space was narrow, it would simply be a path. When made wider, such a space takes on the qualities of a generously proportioned foyer. Benches at the sides will encourage uses beyond mere access, and a collection of potted plants can provide a changing floral display that minimalist plantings don't permit.

*Perennial beds are empty for half the year, but mixed borders, studded with a wide range of evergreens as well as more fleeting flowers, reward the gardener with an ongoing sequence of color and dramatic seasonal change. (Garden of Ernie and Marietta O'Byrne, Eugene, Oregon.)*

Effective structural plantings are often rather minimalist in both form and content. As such, they are less than interesting to plant collectors, who favor variety in every possible situation. With a bit of planning and forethought, it is possible to make a garden room that is both architectural and horticulturally varied. The most effective way to do this is by giving your garden rooms at least one wall that is a mixed hedge.

At Hidcote, Lawrence Johnston made what he called "tapestry hedges," generally combining two kinds of shrubs such as copper beech and hornbeam. This idea can be amplified indefinitely, making garden walls that are tapestries indeed. Even in confined areas, narrow hedges can be woven with sumptuous mixtures of evergreen and deciduous shrubs that will provide ongoing beauty all year-round.

If there is room to allow beds of greater depth, the tapestry hedge can become the backbone of a mixed border. Here, plants of all kinds—shrubs and perennials, vines and bulbs—mingle in tightly interwoven community. By using compact and dwarf plants, an astonishingly rich array can be contrived in very little space.

This sort of garden room makes a delightful outlook for frequently used windows, especially when employed to mask the sight (and muffle the sound) of a busy street. The house wall makes one side, which can itself boast a slim bed in which the usual foundation plants are replaced with handsome, low-growing evergreen shrubs and ground covers laced with seasonal bulbs. The far side is enclosed with a tapestry hedge and mixed border as described. The "floor" may be paved or turfed, and the two shorter walls can be fenced or hedged or entered by arches covered in climbing roses and clematis.

Such a scheme can be large and very complex, but it is equally effective on the smallest scale. Where space is restricted, it is vital to select only plants that offer several seasons of beauty and won't outgrow their position. Compact, dwarf, and border shrubs work best in tiny spaces, as do slender, columnar hedging plants. Any trees used here must be dainty and shapely, growing slowly and remaining handsome all year long.

Many gardeners begin developing garden rooms around the house, using each wall as an anchor and working outward as space permits. Often, each side of the house already has a distinct character which can be developed further. The sunny south becomes a warm, scented haven, floored in culinary herbs and patterned brick and decorated with citrus trees in pots. Here, the enclosing "walls" must be high enough for visual privacy yet low enough to allow in as much light as possible. The six-foot fence allowed by many local building codes will provide ample protection where neighbors are not especially near.

Elsewhere, a fence cap of trelliswork can baffle unwanted views (and viewers). A row of espaliered fruit trees or a lacing of vines along the fence will also help protect your privacy.

The shady north side can be transformed into a green retreat, walled with dense shrubs and floored with flat stones with moss in their chinks. Feathery ferns, wildflowers, and woodland plants predominate here. The quiet drip of water is very appealing in a shady garden room, and also helps mask annoying noises, so mount a recirculating fountain and basin on the house wall. A bench or seat will encourage a meditative restfulness, aided by pots of scented annuals and softly colored foliage plants. An overhead arbor or walkway covered in trellis emphasizes the coziness of this shady haven. For a leafier look, hang baskets of flowers from the beams, or cover them with vines.

To the west, you may want to make a larger, more open garden room where you can bask in the afternoon light and watch the sun set. To keep those long rays out of the house, where they can overheat rooms in summer, screen the windows with some shading shrubs, either as foundation plantings or grown in pots. Feathery bamboos and tall maiden grasses (*Miscanthus*) work well in either situation, creating deliciously cool summer shade yet not blocking light in winter, when it is most appreciated from any direction.

*Enclosure makes even a young garden seem like a place to be in its own right. Where community regulations ban tall fences, trelliswork extensions are often permissible. Planted with vines or left plain, these airy panels baffle views into the garden and muffle street noise as well. (Garden designed by Nancy Hammer, Portico Group, Seattle, Washington.)*

The east side makes a perfect morning room, a place to take that first cup of coffee and enjoy a lazy weekend brunch. This is a great space to make a rose bower, a covered seat with walls draped in climbing roses. Add honeysuckle and jasmine (they can winter over indoors where winters are severe) for additional fragrance.

*Tumbling water creates a lively sound which can be made more intriguing by breaking the water's fall with eccentrically shaped stones. Running water blends with city noises such as traffic and passersby, blending them into a peaceful, natural-sounding music. (Garden designed by John Pruden, Portland International Gardens, Portland, Oregon.)*

Such rooms can be of any size at all, from miniature to grand. They can be furnished to host a crowd or have a single, snug seat for one. They generally provide lovely views from with the house, but can also serve as view extenders within the garden. When a smaller, enclosed space is glimpsed from a larger, more open one, the effect is alluring. It makes us want to explore that half-hidden place, and suggests that the garden is large and complex, whatever its actual size and shape. Such illusions are a valuable part of garden design, particularly when the space we have to work with is not especially interesting in itself.

## GARDEN BONES

Many garden books talk about garden "bones," the architectural elements—living or man-made—which make sense of undefined space. The idea can seem confusing to the uninitiated, but what it really means is structure. Try to imagine what your living room furniture would look like if it were suddenly transported to the middle of a parking lot. Without walls and a ceiling for reference, the arrangement would probably look rather arbitrary. Our garden plants, too, can look irrelevant or out of place when placed in an open, empty yard without apparent reference to anything.

Garden structure comes from those solid things that make reference points for our plants. The hardscape we discussed earlier makes up part of our garden structure. Paths lead both eye and foot, dividing spaces and enticing us into and around the garden. Patios, decks, and terraces are places to delight in the garden, and their edges offer logical places for our garden beds to begin. Trellises, arbors, and pergolas are all focal points which readily invite expansion into beds and borders.

Structure also comes from the enclosure of garden space with fences, walls, or hedges. Enclosures provide visual boundaries, but they also provoke subconscious emotional responses which strongly affect the way we use our garden space. In many yards, a great deal of space is wasted because the overall design does not invite us to use it. Open space can feel particularly unappealing when it is overlooked by neighbors or the street. Because of this, the average front yard is literally never used except when yard maintenance chores are being performed. Many a backyard remains empty as well, particularly those that are open to view from other houses. One time-proven way to make such a yard more attractive (in the sense of drawing us in) is, as we discussed, by creating smaller, enclosed areas within the greater space.

### More Plants for Screening

Those trees and shrubs which are the first plants to consider placing are what gardeners call "bone" plants: structural, usually woody trees and shrubs that lend a young garden shape and definition. Except in mild climates, garden trees are usually deciduous. However, garden shrubs are usually evergreens that can perform their multiple functions all year-round. Thoughtfully chosen and well placed, they become a firm basis for the garden's design, their strong forms clearly dictating the position of subsidiary plants.

Now, very few new gardeners make their first visit to a garden center driven by the desperate desire for garden bones. Indeed, once there, it is practically a sure thing that if the novice plant shopper falls head over heels for something, it won't be a yew or a juniper. Our attention will

*Free-standing trellis units offer climbing plants a chance to roam. Such structures must be overbuilt for safety, especially if they are to hold up plants (large vines can be very heavy). These solid pieces are set on concrete footings which reduce foot rot in the supporting beams. (Garden of Elizabeth Lair, Eugene, Oregon.)*

instead be naturally directed toward plants with more obvious attractions, such as splendid flowers and ornamental fruits.

However, this is a good time to develop better familiarity with those plain Jane bone plants. Though considerably less showy than roses or lilies, the stolid evergreens graciously endow young gardens with considerable strength. After all, our garden rooms or divisions need walls of some kind, and only rarely will they all be hard-edged, man-made ones. To build living green walls, we need to assemble a crew of sturdy evergreens that can screen unwanted views and frame attractive ones.

What is required is a selection of site adaptive, easy-care plants that will size up quickly, yet not outgrow their position. Unless you are planning an utterly formal garden, look for plants which mature in a range of sizes. The largest bone shrubs may top out at ten to fifteen feet, medium range shrubs at eight to twelve feet, and the smallest at six to eight feet. These should be plants that will maintain a pleasing natural shape for many years, requiring little or no regular pruning.

That's a tall order, but luckily, plenty of evergreens fit the bill. You can find good candidates in a number of ways. To start with, consult local nursery folk, and visit lots of different nurseries, both big chain garden centers and small specialty places. Go to the library and seek out

*House or garage walls can look blank or intimidating at close range. The effect can be softened by covering them with trellised plants, or by turning them into a display area for collections of birdhouses, garden tools, or artworks. (Garden designed by Linda Terhark, Oceanside, Oregon.)*

*A combination of evergreen hedging and edging plants give this attractive cottage garden a tidy, well-filled appearance in any season. Sheared hedges imply a certain formality of design, but by using naturally compact and shapely evergreens for edging and low interior hedging, the gardener minimizes maintenance. (Garden of Valerie Murray, Victoria, British Columbia.)*

good regional reference books which offer listings of appropriate evergreen plants. Once you have some attractive choices in mind, you can then tour public gardens, parks, and arboreta to see what your growing list of possible screening plants will look like in maturity.

*Best Bets for Perimeter Hedges and Bones*

Thanks to hard-working hybridizers like David Leach, we can now select among dozens of handsome, hardy rhododendrons, all of which make excellent screeners. One of my favorites is 'Lodestar' (zone 5, to 10 feet), a chunky, well-furnished shrub with glossy leaves and enormous trusses of white flowers with pale golden hearts. These blend beautifully into gentle springtime color schemes, as will those of 'Hong Kong' (zone 5, to 10 feet), which are imperial yellow touched with lacquer red. For perimeter plantings, consider taller, arborescent forms like 'Sir Charles Lemon' (zone 6, 12–20 feet). This big guy has large, dark green leaves lined with cinnamon-orange fur (*R. indumentum*) and topped with generous clusters of buttery yellow flowers that smell delicately, and appropriately, of lemons.

Most conifers are beautiful, mannerly, and easy to please. Where winters are severe, the few broad-leaved evergreens that survive can look pretty ratty during the colder months. In such places, needled evergreens are always the bone plants of choice, but their many graces make these sturdy plants welcome in warmer gardens as well.

For instance, narrow, columnar Western red cedar (*Juniperus scopulorum*) 'Wichita Blue' (zone 4, 15–20 feet) is a knockout, both in youth and in maturity. Steely blue-gray and fluffy as a cloud, its color and texture complement an enormous range of plants, making it a natural for back of-the-border duty. Though it thickens a bit at midlife, it remains upright and shapely for many years.

Bluer still is Eastern red cedar (*Juniperus virginiana*) 'Manhattan Blue' (zone 4, 10–15 feet), another fine columnar form that makes a lovely background plant in mixed borders. Paired with lustrous green cherry laurel (*Prunus laurocerasus*, zone 6, a 10–12 foot shrub or 18-foot tree), it makes a sumptuously textured tapestry hedge.

Among my favorites for screening in warm gardens is the admirable Pacific wax myrtle (*Myrica californica,* zone 7, 20–30 feet). Upright and densely clad, its slim, leathery leaves have a bronzed, healthy sheen all year-round. It tolerates windy sites and adapts well to dry or acid soils. Wax myrtle loves full sun, but performs well in light or partial shade.

Another good performer is laurustinus (*Viburnum tinus,* zone 7, to 12 feet). This chunky evergreen is covered in small, glossy, fine-textured leaves all year. In spring, it produces copious sprays of softly pink and white flowers followed by metallic blue berries in fall. No matter where you live, you will discover hundreds of likely candidates to choose from. Be guided by manners and looks in maturity as well as in the nursery pot, and you will soon develop a worthy palette of plants to give your garden good bones.

### *Garden Room Enclosure: Interior Hedging*

How you enclose each section of the garden will depend in part on how you plan to use it. Once you decide which activities best suit each

*A tall holly hedge created enclosure at the expense of precious space. The top was left leafy, but the base was pruned hard, creating gaps in the visual barrier. These were filled with fencing, allowing room for the tree trunks to merge sculpturally into the slats. (Lonesomeville, Portland, Oregon.)*

available area, you can think about ways to create appropriate and practical visual boundaries between them. For the outer "walls" of the garden perimeter, traditional choices include evergreen or deciduous hedges as well as fences or walls. Where any or all of these are already in place, the garden is half made from the start.

In new gardens, however, there is often no enclosure at all. If there is a hedge, it is probably so young as to be purely incipient. We have already looked at ways to create temporary enclosure while a young perimeter hedge is growing up. Because large hedges require several years to size up, they should be planted early on, but backed up by a secondary screen or visual baffle.

Common, quick-growing hedge plants will be relatively inexpensive and are frequent sale items at large nursery chains. Sometimes these are terrific bargains, but before you spring for a hundred baby pine trees, ask yourself a few questions. Do you want an evergreen hedge, or could a dense row of twiggy deciduous shrubs work just as well? Evergreen hedge plants are usually significantly more expensive than deciduous ones, but if you aren't out in the yard much during the winter, the extra protection may not be worth the extra expense. Ask yourself too whether you want to trim your hedge or not. In the city, formal homes and garden designs seem to demand clipped hedges. However, tightly spaced evergreens with a naturally upright habit can look quite dapper even when unclipped. In some situations, notably in suburban or country gardens, an excess of clipped hedges may look pretentious, while a shaggy row of unsheared arborvitae will make a convincing visual link with native trees and shrubs nearby.

Indeed, untrimmed hedges are not necessarily casual or sloppy-looking; much depends on the plants you choose. Evergreen mountain laurel (*Kalmia latifolia*, zone 4, to 30 feet) has a naturally tidy habit, and needs only occasional minor pruning to maintain a formal appearance. Arching bridal wreath spirea (*Spiraea* × *vanhouttei*, zone 4, to 6 feet) has enough strength of form that a wide row of it appears equally charming when flanking a driveway circle before a country house or lining a broad walkway in front of a formal town house.

The next question will further refine your possible choices: Does the available hedge space offer adequate width for large shrubs, or should you be looking for narrow, tightly columnar plants? In general, you can assume that a mature hedge will be about as wide as it is tall. If you want the little hedge between the vegetable patch and the swing set to be four feet high, you'll need to allocate a four-foot-wide strip for it. For a twelve-foot tall front hedge, you'll need to leave six feet of clear space on both sides of the baby hedge to allow for future growth.

If you realize that such a big hedge will encroach on the sidewalk and fill the entire front yard, you may prefer to enclose that area with a

*Where little room is left between walkways and beds, hedges can be made of narrow columnar plants with little lateral spread. Hedges that are clipped for many years grow congested unless they are periodically thinned, removing excess branches to allow more light and air to reach the trunk. This keeps plants healthy and promotes vigorous new growth. (Portland Japanese Garden, Portland, Oregon.)*

fence instead. As a good rule of thumb, anything you plant should remain on your property even in maturity. A hedge placed where it will intrude on public or private property stands a good chance of getting more of a trimming than you want it to, either from irate neighbors or a zealous city pruning crew.

The next step is to take all these factors into consideration and get yourself some regionally accurate advice. Many general garden books in this country are written with the Northeast in mind. If you live in Florida or Omaha, take such books with a grain of salt. Advice gleaned at your local nursery is likely to be more trustworthy. Check, too, with your county extension service agent for a listing of Master Gardner clinics. These folks train long and hard to solve a slew of common garden problems. Their advice is free, and often backed up by researchers at a local university.

Once you have decided what you need, it becomes relatively simple to select an appropriate hedge plant that suits your situation. Now you can go shopping. When we were assembling screening plants, we looked for an assortment of shapes and sizes. Shrubs that are to be arranged in naturalistic groups look far more interesting when there is some variation of size. Hedges, however, demand uniformity. In this case, we want plants that match each other as closely as possible in height and girth.

Even if you are making tapestry or mixed hedges involving several kinds of plants, the result will be more pleasing when all the shrubs are similar in size and shape. When a hedge mixture offers too much variety, it creates visual chaos. Instead of blending into a solid backdrop, the mixed plants remain stubbornly separate, offering the eye a distracting jumble of forms.

Tapestry hedges often appeal to plant lovers who prefer variety over repetition. One good way to indulge plant lust without spoiling the design of the garden is to keep the main green walls simple, but make the smaller, interior hedges out of the most interesting plants you can find. In smaller spaces, you can go wild, combining striking backdrop shrubs in satisfyingly creative

*Grassy areas become soggy in winter, but open courtyards paved with gravel remain dry and inviting even during the quieter months. The backdrop of trees and shrubs soften the edge of the garden and make it appear larger than it really is. (Garden designed by Nancy Hammer, Portico Group, Seattle, Washington.)*

compositions. Because the overall area involved is not great, there won't be room to create chaos, since only a few compact or dwarf plants will fit. In a tiny garden room, a plain hedge can look pretty boring, but a vividly mixed tapestry of shrubs makes a fascinating wall that never looks dull.

Choicer shrubs can be harder to find in quantity and matching sizes, but the search is delightful, involving as it does trips to many and various nurseries. Indeed, unless both your budget and time line are unlimited, it will definitely prove most practical to settle for standard hedging plants where your garden plan requires large quantities of them. Reserve the unusual (and more expensive) hedge plants for places where even small groupings will be most appreciated.

Even ardent plant collectors may decide to opt for plain hedges when they realize what splendidly understated backdrops they make. Where complex plantings are to be framed, the simplicity of plain yew or privet is highly complementary. Here, a long run of brightly colored leaves or wildly textured greenery can become overwhelming, distracting the eye from the beds and borders that are intended to be the visual heart of the garden.

On the other hand, there are places where such a hedge becomes a work of art. When paired with potent modern architecture, a visually aggressive hedge becomes as compellingly eye-catching as the building it encloses. In such a situation, a garden design combining extreme simplicity and boldness will be most successful anyway, and an extravagantly woven tapestry hedge will look terrific.

**LITTLE HEDGES** Within the garden, low hedges are often used to divide spaces into rooms, to frame vegetable or rose gardens, and to edge beds as well as paths and walkways. These inner hedges can be as simple as a shaggy row of unpruned lavender or as contrived as an arrow-straight line of sheared boxwoods, depending on the style and feeling you want to evoke.

Where a low interior garden hedge is meant to guide the feet but allow the eye to see beyond the barrier into an adjacent garden area, compact shrubs such as boxleaf honeysuckle (*Lonicera nitida*, zone 7, to 6 feet) or one of the shorter privets (*Ligustrum* species, zones 4–5) can be kept to heights of three or four feet by annual clipping. Those who want a looser, unclipped low hedge can consider dwarf barberries (*Berberis* species, zones 5–6), glossy Japanese hollies (*Ilex crenata* forms, zones 5–6), or evergreen sheep laurel (*Kalmia angustifolia*, zone 2), which rarely exceeds three feet and always looks tidy.

Dozens of small shrubs, evergreen or deciduous, are suitable for interior hedges. By visiting gardens and nurseries and making notes about attractive small shrubs, you can build up a list of candidates to use in your own garden. Points to consider are the ultimate height and width of the

*Unclipped hedges can be draped with climbing vines and decorated like living walls. Here, a lacy clematis loops gaily through the backdrop hedge, brightening its blankness with a wealth of scented blossoms and silken seedheads. If hedges are to be clipped, choose companion vines that can be trimmed back hard each year. (Garden designed by Dulcy Mahar, Portland, Oregon.)*

unpruned plant and how frequently it requires clipping to remain tidy. If your chosen shrub produces pretty flowers and fruits, find out whether it will still do so when constantly pruned. (Some shrubs only flower on new wood, so each time you cut away the young growth, you are also removing potential flowers.)

Edging shrubs like dwarf boxwood or lavender may be clipped or left natural in shape. Even if you plan to shear your hedges, you can minimize the work by selecting dwarf plants. Because they grow slowly, the amount of control you will need to exert to keep your edging hedges looking trim is reduced. Where space is tight, there may not be room for unclipped shrubs unless they have a naturally upright, narrow form. In such a spot, you will probably need to do a light annual pruning no matter what kind of plant you pick for the job.

Again, one good solution is to choose slimmer plants. For taller hedges, Irish junipers (*Juniperus communis* 'Stricta' or 'Hibernica', zone 2, 12–20 feet) are good choices where soils are poor, for they tolerate both heavy clay and sand, as well as persistent dampness or drought. They take up relatively little ground space, maturing between twelve and twenty feet in height but rarely exceeding five feet in width. The even skinnier ones called 'Skyrocket' (*J. scopulorum*, zone 3, 10–15 feet) are almost as adaptable and seldom get wider than two feet across, even when reaching their ultimate height.

#### FINDING THE MAGIC NUMBER

Unfortunately, there is no magic formula for calculating how many hedge plants you will need. Obviously, you will determine the right number when you know how long the hedge needs to be and how closely the plants should be spaced. This last, however, depends on several variables: What kind of plants you have chosen; how big they are; what size you want the hedge to be; and what kind of soil and conditions you can offer them.

For example, a shady site is less than ideal for most hedge plants, and they will need to be spaced a bit closer and pruned harder to get them to fatten up properly. If you have a sunny run and fine soil, you will be able to space your plants further apart and still get fairly quick coverage. If your hedge plants are five-gallon shrubs, you will space them further apart than if you are using gallon-size plants or whips (unbranched cuttings).

Any hedge handbook will give you guidance on the calculating process, as will the nursery that sells you the plants. Common sense helps, too; if you have decided on 'Skyrocket' junipers and you know they may not be quite two feet wide at maturity, you can safely set them on eighteen-inch centers. If you buy young 'Skyrocket' trees between six and eight feet high, this spacing will give you a dense, interwoven barrier quite quickly.

If you have room, you can arrange a double hedge in staggered rows for almost instant coverage. This way, the plants in the second row mask the gaps left between those in the first. With slender, columnar trees, even a double row takes up less space than an ordinary hedge. A fifteen-foot hedge of beech or laurel would be at least fifteen feet wide, but a double hedge of fifteen-foot junipers (the slimmest sorts) can be fitted into a mere four-foot strip.

How closely you can space your hedge plants also depends somewhat on the kind of soil you have. Some plants will thrive in rich soil, but others will get overly lush and be more prone to diseases than when grown in leaner soil. Before you fertilize the hedge row, find out what kind of soil and feeding your chosen plant needs. Most common hedge plants do best in ordinary garden soil that has been improved with soil-building amendments rather than fertilizers. Compost, aged manure, and rotted sawdust are all good for promoting root growth without encouraging excessively fast growth.

Fast growth seems desirable in a hedge, and so it is, yet too much can lead to problems. In the garden as elsewhere, steady, unchecked growth gives better long-term results than quick spurts boosted by artificial stimulants. What's more,

plants that grow extremely fast often don't live very long. If you aren't planning to stay put for very long, maybe you don't mind that drawback, but it's amazing how quickly the years fly by. Plants that have a fifteen- or twenty-year healthy life span, like certain poplars and some false cypress (*Chamaecyparis lawsoniana*), may size up quickly, but when they start dying off, they leave unsightly gaps in your hedge that are impossible to fill properly.

*Tight spaces require tight shearing, so select plants that tolerate frequent cutting back. Here, the formal line of the flowing staircase is echoed by the strict geometry of the enclosing hedge. To reduce the workload while retaining the essential quality of this handsome planting, substitute plants with a natural formal habit, such as Thuja occidentalis 'Douglas Pyramidal'. (Garden designed by Pamela Burton, Santa Monica, California.)*

**CHOOSING HEDGE PLANTS THAT WILL WORK FOR YOU** Hedges are traditionally made with adaptable, vigorous plants like privet and honey locust. These plants are tough troopers that are not easily discouraged. This is important, because hedge plants are subjected to repeated stresses to make them conform to our desires. First they are planted very close together, causing root competition almost immediately. Next, they are cut back hard to encourage bushy growth at the base and keep the leader (main trunk) from getting too tall. Through their life, their new growth is removed almost constantly. Unless the hedge is carefully sheared so that it is considerably wider at the base than at the top, the lower limbs are shaded by the upper ones, making them weak and scrawny. Only the strongest plants can take this kind of abuse with aplomb. It makes sense, therefore, that the plants which do will also need a considerable amount of restraining. For instance, you can count on shearing a happy privet hedge two or three or even more times each year.

Unless you have reliable garden help or really enjoy clipping hedges, you will probably prefer hedge plants that do much of the work for you. These include any plant, deciduous or evergreen, that has a handsome natural shape

*Staggered rows of mixed evergreens create a lush, irregularly tiered backdrop with an attractively naturalistic look. Combining a young hedge with a plain wooden fence provides instant privacy and shelters the maturing plants from wind and traffic fumes. (Garden designed by Jeff Glander, Tacoma, Washington.)*

and neat habit (manner of growth). When made into hedges, they will probably require a modicum of shaping at first, but when properly spaced and appropriately fed, these natural beauties will fill in quickly and do their job for many years without much help from you.

What they won't do is provide instant screening. Spaced to allow for full, natural shapes, such plants may take several years to fill in enough to become effective as a hedge. Where time is not of the essence and you are planting for the future, this is not a problem. Where you want both future beauty and present coverage, coupling the young hedge with a fence of some kind will meet both needs.

Another excellent way to provide quick coverage is by pairing young hedge shrubs with large grasses. Spaced on three- or four-foot centers, five-gallon plants of tall eulalia grass (*Miscanthus sinensis*, zone 4, to 10 feet) will create a visually effective boundary in a single season. Indeed, many of the big grasses are potent enough in form to be used this way. They don't hold their shape in winter and take a while to leaf out in spring, but anywhere that a summery screen is wanted, big grasses will do the trick inexpensively and in short order.

All across the country, needled evergreens with a trim natural shape are splendid candidates for unclipped hedges. As mentioned, the slenderest of them will fit comfortably into very narrow spaces, making them obvious choices in smaller gardens. Those classed as pyramidal begin life skinny but bulge at the base with age. These have the advantage of dense coverage for the bottom ten feet of hedge and airier tops, allowing in light while effectively blocking unwanted views. Pyramidal hedge plants work best where there's plenty of room for them to bulk out.

Where space is unlimited, nearly any sort of evergreen tree can be used. If no space constraint exists, space your hedge plants generously, allowing room for them to develop their full natural shapes. This will take several years, so if quicker cover is wanted, set the trees in double rows and let them rip. In a couple of seasons, you will have a magnificent hedge, bushy and beautiful, which provides a lifetime of enclosure with very little care.

In mild climates, any of a number of mannerly, shapely broad-leaved evergreens can be used for hedging. Camellias, rhododendrons, viburnums, and laurels all offer narrow and lastingly handsome forms which will do hedge duty well and without causing a lot of extra work for the gardener. In either case, check your choice with a reliable regional resource or two before investing in a whole hedge-worth of expensive plants. If your area has suitable soil and climate and offers no pests and diseases to plague your chosen plants, then you can be pretty sure that your hedge will repay your efforts in installing it many times over.

### When Walls Will and Won't Work

Those luscious English garden books are usually full of billowy borders backed up by tastefully crumbling walls that are at least a few centuries old. Not surprisingly, English designers are quick to instruct North Americans to add "proper walls" to our gardens, explaining that our typical garden designs are short on enclosure *and* structure. This is quite true, yet enclosing walls are not always practical on this side of the water.

For one thing, walls of any kind are quite expensive to have built. You can of course elect to make them yourself, but be prepared to expend a good deal of time and effort as well as an astonishing amount of money. Still, if you are one of those people who find stonework meditative and relaxing, this may be an excellent way to enclose your garden.

If you haven't yet tried the art of wall building but think it sounds attractive, don't start with a major project. Try your hand on a few interior garden walls, the kind which separate beds or main planting areas. These are smaller and lower than a garden's outer walls, and are rarely the first thing visitors will see.

If your little wall is not a success, it's easy enough to disguise any shortcomings by draping your handiwork generously with enthusiastically cascading wall plants. Indeed, this is a splendid way to disguise walls made from less than lovely materials. Well-draped, and with all its chinks stuffed with creepers and spillers, a wall made of broken-up sidewalk can be hard to tell from a wall of raw stone.

Another point is that modern walls almost never have the charm of a beautifully aged one. The raw red of new brick is a far cry from the mellow richness of antique ones. Old brick provides a soothing background for a host of colors, but new brick must be partnered with

*Stonework can create a beautiful garden enclosure, and if well-constructed, stone walls provide both visual privacy and an opportunity to create more planting beds. However, the process takes time and large stones are difficult for amateurs to work with. It's best to start with a small project in an out-of-the way part of the garden. (Garden of Lucy and Fred Hardiman, Portland, Oregon.)*

great care or you end up with extremely regrettable combinations that are impossible to overlook or disguise. Though concrete is unobjectionable in color, there is no way to make new concrete blocks look anything like ancient stone. The kindest thing you can do about a wall built with them is to cover it with plants as quickly as possible.

New stonework made with beautiful local rock can look lovely almost at once, especially when not slathered with quantities of brilliantly white grouting. Cut stone walls are as difficult to build as brickwork, and they emphatically do not make a good first project. Simple, unmortared walls built with roughly shaped rocks are by far the easiest for amateurs to attempt with any degree of success. However, even these require a fair amount of attention to detail to look right. Those with the knack find choosing and setting wall stones almost effortless, and their results are generally happy.

Those who find such work tedious and fidgety will be better off hiring help. So will those who, like me, need to spare their hands and wrists. Gardeners with arthritis or carpal tunnel syndrome will probably derive more pleasure (and less pain) from planting their gardens than building walls. Personally, I love the look of stone walls as much as the idea of making them myself. However, I inevitably overestimate my ability to juggle heavy stones and end up dropping an amazing number of them on my fingers. Even when my work is fairly successful, I end up paying for it for days afterward with stiff hands and sore wrists. Though admitting defeat is never fun, I now hire less klutzy friends to make my walls and steps, consoling myself with the realization that I am boosting the economy.

*Enclosure from Fencing*

For many folks, fencing proves to be the most practical and affordable means of achieving enclosure. Even the simplest fence can be costly when made with top-quality materials. However, there are plenty of attractive options that won't break a moderate budget. If you want to build it yourself, you cut the price of any fence dramatically.

In most cases, fencing is relatively simple to install even for those without experience. If the slope of the land changes a good deal or it is too rocky to dig post holes easily, you may want to hire professionals to set the posts for you. You can then add the stringers and the boarding on your own schedule.

Fencing has its own rules, and it's a good idea to borrow a few fencing handbooks from the

*This Asian-inspired fencing has gently stepped lines which look in keeping with the naturalistic plantings. Where straight edges might appear harsh and out of place, irregularly shaped fencing achieves enclosure without jolting the eye. (Garden of Robin Hopper and Judi Dyelle, Metchosin, British Columbia.)*

library before finalizing your design. Practical designs will take into consideration such factors as the weight of each panel or section, which also determines how far apart the posts can be set. Most large hardware stores offer prebuilt sections of inexpensive fencing in various patterns. You can alter the look of a very plain fence by topping it with long, narrow trellis panels called fence caps. Alternating solid and openwork trellis sections can also make a simple fence pattern more intriguing.

As we've seen, the most complete and immediate garden enclosure may be achieved through a combination of means. An inexpensive fence can be put up in just a few days by amateur handy-folk. A young hedge can then be planted in front (or behind), to provide greater protection in time.

If your yard is enclosed by a chain-link fence, you already know that this kind of fencing provides practical enclosure without the psychological benefits. A few modifications can alter both its appearance and emotional effect quite dramatically. Chain-link fences are among the homeliest of boundary makers, but take heart; there is hope. Here in the Northwest, a classic remodel involves threading slim strips of cedar through the links. They look nicest in long diagonals, but can be arranged lots of ways, including weaving them through each other as well as the fence. The cedar weathers to a gentle gray that complements any and all plants. The strips also give creepers and climbers a toehold, helping to clothe the fence more quickly with living drapery.

Such sheltering curtains should be made from sturdy, wind-tolerant plants. If your region is warm enough, you can select evergreen vines like English ivy

## BAMBOO FENCING

*Bamboo fencing can make understated divisions of space within the garden or subtly guide wandering feet away from an easily damaged mossy bank. (Built by Fred White at the Portland Japanese Garden, Portland, Oregon.)*

*Woven bamboo is very strong and holds up well over time, especially when the bottom pieces do not touch the damp ground. (Built by Fred White at the Portland Japanese Garden, Portland, Oregon.)*

*Relatively inexpensive, bamboo is also quite easy to work with. Whole or split stems can be combined in a multitude of patterns to create immediate, short-term or longer-lasting fencing. Wire or leather ties can replace nails or screws and give the fencing a more traditional appearance. Bamboo stems can be cut to fit right on the job site, making it easy to work around rocks or mature tree trunks. (Built by Fred White at the Portland Japanese Garden, Portland, Oregon.)*

(*Hedera helix*, zone 5, to 50 feet), which builds into very dense coverage over time. Like many rampant plants, ivy is slow to get started, putting most of its energy into roots for the first year or so. This makes it seem as if nothing is happening, but be patient. Just keep the ivy's root zone free of invading grasses and before long it will be leaping upward as fast as you like.

A chain-link fence also provides a perfect matrix for woven ivy patterns. Thanks to the regular spacing of the links, it's easy to train ivy into formal patterns reminiscent of espaliered fruit trees. Diamonds, lozenges, and other geometrical shapes are child's play even for the novice. Artistic gardeners can create charming ivy-based designs along the order of petit-point work or cross-stitch embroidery. Combine ivies in several colors to make a living plaid, or mix shapes for a subtle study in textures. This last will prove most practical where the fence is to be the background for a flower border, while a more elaborate pattern will be lastingly pleasing in a smaller area without competitive plantings.

Other evergreen vines can also be used, such as Chinese *Clematis armandii* (zone 7, to 100 feet), a powerfully handsome creature with long, slim leaves that make a dramatic background for summery border plants. This clematis produces bunches of white or pink fragrant flowers in early spring. It can be trained sideways nearly as far as you like by securing the soft new growth with flexible plant ties. All clematis resent handling, so be firm but gentle in redirecting those long, waving arms. This striking vine is often used to frame cottages or smother an unsightly garage, but it does fence duty with flare, filling in fast and blooming well when young. Because it blooms on old wood, don't do any pruning until after the spring flowering is over. If you don't mind an open fence in winter, you can weave a scented tapestry hedge using honeysuckles (*Lonicera* species) and climbing roses. Add a few clematis for spring and summer color, and you'll find your ugly fence has become a true beauty. To speed things up, lace it with annual vines like scented sweet peas, blazing scarlet runner beans, or the ornamental hyacinth bean (*Lablab purpureus*), with fragrant purple flowers and vivid burgundy pods.

### *How to Frame the Scenery*

There are also times when partial enclosure is most desirable. This can be achieved with a combination of the techniques already mentioned, or with green architecture. Most good screening plants also make good view framers. Solid, shapely plants that screen without hogging too much space are invaluable for both purposes. Well placed, such plants assist us in creating lovely gardens unmarred by road signs or the neighbor's double-wide trailer home. Hopefully, after reading about making and screening views in

*Pairs of slim, columnar trees are a classic view-framing treatment. In the garden's interior, this device can divide an ornamental area of the yard from a more practical part or announce the entrance to a garden room. Placed in the perimeter plantings, it might capture a glimpse of a distant mountain, a cityscape, or the shimmering sea. (Israelit garden, designed by Michael Schultz, Portland, Oregon.)*

Chapter 3, your map also indicates more scenic vistas to emphasize. Whether such views involve a magnificent tree nearby or a distant mountain, they nearly always benefit from judicious framing.

Usually, the most effective way to enhance a desirable view is by editing it, setting it within a defining (or refining) framework. This can be done architecturally, with cut-out fencing, arbors, trelliswork, and so forth. Framing can also be beautifully done with trees and shrubs. This simpler approach is often the most practical (plants being relatively inexpensive) and often feels more in keeping with the style of naturalistic gardens.

Naturally, views can be framed with almost any kind of plants. Think of the famous laburnum walk at Barnsley House, where trees are trained over metal arches to form a long arbor. A similar effect could be achieved with vines, evergreen or deciduous, trained over metal or wooden frames of any shape.

*A temporary framing effect can be stylishly accomplished with bold perennials like these sturdy rudbeckias. Tall grasses would make a similarly strong yet softer-looking framework that would remain in beauty over a long season. (Garden designed by Nancy Hammer, Portico Group, Seattle, Washington.)*

While framing plants can be deciduous, evergreens have a solid presence that contributes to the garden's structure all year-round. In colder climates, the choices will be limited to conifers and deciduous trees and shrubs. In milder areas, suitable broadleaf evergreens expand the options a good deal.

In general, view framers are tall and slim. Like the rest of us, some plants that start out with ideal proportions tend to spread a bit in middle age. This sorrow can be avoided by selecting shrubs and trees that maintain their perfection of line for many years. We also want to find plants that size up quickly enough to do their job when fairly young, yet know when to stop.

Plants that mature between fifteen and twenty feet in height are ideal for smaller gardens where space is limited. Some of my own favorite columnar evergreens are junipers like the narrow, Chinese blue column juniper (*Juniperus chinensis* 'Columnaris', 12–15 feet); skinny, grass green Irish juniper (*J. communis* 'Stricta', 12–20 feet); or slim, leaf green Western red cedar (*J. scopulorum* 'Cologreen', 12–18 feet).

There are some fetchingly spirelike deciduous trees as well, including such charmers as the maiden-hair ginkgo (*Ginkgo biloba* var. *fastigiata*, zone 4, to 120 feet), which turns pale gold in autumn. (Just make sure you get a male tree because the female's fruit smells powerfully revolting.) Slim mountain ash (*Sorbus aucuparia* 'Fastigiata' zone 2, to 45 feet), Sargent or Japanese cherry (*Prunus sargentii* 'Columnaris', zone 2, to 60 feet; *P. serrulata* 'Amanogawa', zone 5, to 26 feet), and white birch (*Betula pendula* 'Fastigiata', zone 2, to 60 feet), all have lovely, slender forms that remain tightly columnar. Placed in pairs on either side of a wonderful view, any of these trees will create a handsome frame to complete your natural picture.

FIVE

# GETTING DOWN TO EARTH

## BIG PROJECTS COME FIRST

*Now that your information gathering is done and you've had time to mull over some of the principles underlying garden enclosure, it's time for some synthesis. We have* reached the intermediate stage of plan development, when those bubbles and blobs get combined with your written ideas and dreams. Pull out that tattered map one more time and take a good look at it. It's remarkable how much more information is there than when you started, and how much better acquainted you are with the possibilities offered by your property.

It's also remarkable how that knowledge frees your creative mind. As you record all those dry facts, fresh ideas come bubbling up, suggesting new ways to

*Some settings confront the gardener with the immediate need to stabilize a slope or regrade a steep cliff. Hardscape and regrade work that requires machinery (such as this large-scale rock work) must be completed before any plantings are attempted. In time, vines and creepers will soften the raw look of the new stone, which will darken as it oxidizes. Within a few years, its color will more closely match the native beach stone. (Garden of Elaine and Dave Whitehead, Saanich, British Columbia.)*

treat that empty yard. Exciting projects have presented themselves, along with solutions to design difficulties. You still may not be completely certain about how every last part of the yard should be used, but by now, you probably have an excellent sense of overview.

Though the process of walking and studying the area you have to work with seems lengthy, it is extremely productive. The very act of paying so much attention to our available space coaxes it to reveal its potential uses quite freely. The optimal location for garden access is now obvious, and you know where you need more privacy, a bit of screening, or some shade. The sunniest spots have been designated for garden beds and other popular uses, while practical activities like composting, storing trash cans, and doggy exercise have been relegated to places with the least desirable qualities (in gardening terms).

Garden-making, like any other complex enterprise, is best done in stages. By now, your map is covered with possible projects. Unless your budget for both time and money is unlimited, those projects will need to be scheduled over many months, or even years. Before deciding how to organize your development schedule, consider which projects you will need help with, which will take the most time and effort, and which will be the most rewarding in terms of use.

It can be puzzling to assign priorities when every plan is appealing, but a few rules of thumb can help you decide which should come first. Emotionally, our strongest wish is often to make a flower or vegetable bed. Though many of us can't wait to start growing our favorite flowers or foods, it often proves most practical to take care of major construction projects like terracing a slope or building a deck before developing purely ornamental parts of the garden.

Happily, there is no reason not to create a small flower bed or two right away, so long as these infant plantings don't block access for any heavy equipment that bigger projects may necessitate. Ideally, you should also position temporary beds where you can visit and appreciate them easily, but where they won't be in the way of all the coming and going with cart and barrow that the first stages of garden-making necessitate. In small spaces where this is challenging indeed, a set of window boxes can serve to hold those longed-for flowers until the ground spaces can be properly prepared.

Personally, I always give myself this kind of treat, making at least one starter bed and packing it full of plants for all seasons. The immediate rewards of that initial bed help me to be more patient with the development stage. Once I have someplace to get my hands in the soil, I can return to the discipline of the design process with fuller attention.

In this chapter, we will discuss how to go about reconstructing or reshaping your property, the pros and cons of hiring outside help, and finally, we will do more thinking about the proper placement of the garden bone structures, both architectural and natural.

The other elements that will make up your garden (such as garden rooms, paths, and planting beds) can be done later or in stages, but it's important to get those trees and big shrubs in place as soon as practically possible, when access is relatively unlimited. The same can be said of enclosing walls and trelliswork, and patios or terraces, as well as water features such as ponds or small pools that might require some excavation. Again, there's no hurry about deciding

*Projects which demand bulldozers and excavators come first. Changes of grade, deep trenching for drainage, and the installation of large decks or patios all come early on the to-do list. (Garden designed by Konrad Gauder, Vancouver, Washington.)*

*Where the fall of land is considerable, a combination of steps and terracing makes steep slopes more usable. Switchbacks keep the hill climb from becoming too steep, and graveled level areas make restful seating areas that can be planted more heavily over time if desired. (Garden designed by John Pruden, Portland International Gardens, Portland, Oregon.)*

exactly how to develop parts of the yard that are ready to be gardened, but this is definitely the time to decide what, if anything, needs to be done about reshaping your land.

## MAKING THE EARTH MOVE

Once you know just where you want to place all the major features and important plants in your garden, you can start to implement your overall master plan. This is when a lot of people panic, especially when the master plan doesn't seem to be so well developed as all that. Don't forget, back in the introduction, we discussed the value of reading the whole book before actually doing anything. Seeing the way each part of the process fits together will give you an overview of the development plan, just as mapmaking has given you an overview of the way you want to use your space. When you come back to this point after reading beyond it, it will feel far less overwhelming.

Making a garden is a big job, but it does not have to be a particularly difficult one. Taken in one huge lump, it can seem daunting indeed, but when we break it down into stages, the doing of each piece feels far more manageable. In practical terms, this means that only the major projects need to be fully developed at this point. It doesn't matter whether the less critical ones are still sketchy or still embryonic, so long as you have done your ground work on the big ones.

The largest jobs, such as creating soil banks or berms, leveling lawns, regrading slopes, and so forth, should be accomplished first. Many yards won't need any reconstruction at all, or will have just a few small reshaping projects that can easily be tackled without professional assistance.

However, the lots surrounding new construction are not uncommonly left in fairly raw condition. Poor subsoil may be barely covered with struggling turf, perhaps eroded in places by water runoff from badly graded slopes. Inadequate drainage ditches may fail to carry away excess water, leaving soggy spots that need to be properly drained. Important sections of the yard may be too steep to mow safely, too irregular to be used with comfort, too flat for visual interest, or

*Where changes of grade only involve a few feet, they can be managed without bringing in heavy equipment. A simple flight of steps, wide and shallow, makes a lovely place to sit and look down on the lower garden. Dense plantings reduce the likelihood of soil slippage on the side banks. (Garden of Elizabeth Lair, Eugene, Oregon.)*

### HIRING A CONTRACTOR

If you aren't inclined to make the earth move yourself, call around and get a few estimates from local contractors. Small jobs don't always interest big companies, but keep looking and you'll find plenty of good choices. Garden centers and nurseries can often recommend skilled amateur machine operators who have their own equipment. Many a weekend earth mover does as good a job as a full-timer. Make sure, though, that whomever you hire has good insurance (no joke). Don't be shy about asking for references, and do follow up on them. Ask for both recent and older customer's names, so you can see whether their work was lastingly acceptable.

What's more, a highly experienced earth mover can give you invaluable advice about how best to shape your land to suit your purposes and ideas. If the guy (it's nearly always a guy) shakes his head and looks dubious after you explain your desires, treat that as a red flag. Ask him exactly how he would do it and listen up. You may not want to adopt his advice wholesale, but most definitely do take it under consideration. If he says a certain angle of slope will be unstable or too steep to mow or whatever, it probably will.

too open and unprotected to attract frequent use. If so, you will probably want to think about regrading, building up substantial raised beds on several levels, or having a privacy berm constructed along the roadside or between you and the neighbors.

In any case, the need for remedial earth moving is usually quite obvious. If after walking your property, you are baffled as to where you might need to rework it, you probably don't. If, however, you found any areas that deter active use because they are awkwardly shaped or sloped, they are candidates for some serious earth work.

Confident, mechanically skilled, and adventurous people may find do-it-yourself earth moving tremendous fun. My whole family had a delightful time with a rental Bobcat, smoothing out the driveway and turning a rough meadow into a baseball field. The house got hit only once, but not so hard that anything serious got broken (and it wasn't one of the kids running that Bobcat, either). I even found it kind of peaceful to do without the telephone for a few days. (Those little digger-scooper arms Bobcats have can be raised up a lot higher than you might think.)

It took me a while to get the courage to try it myself, but once behind the controls, the taste of raw power was pretty heady. After years of double-digging beds by hand, it felt amazingly fun to move yards of soil in mere minutes. I still had to do all the fine tuning of shaping my new beds by hand, but a more skillful machine operator can leave them almost in plantable condition.

All in all, our family Bobcat session was a positive one. If we made a few mistakes, no lasting harm was done, and everybody felt they had gained a valuable and enjoyable experience. In a single weekend, we got through a lot of heavy work at relatively little expense. We also saved money by using free fill dirt provided by city work crews. It wasn't good enough for garden soil, but was fine for building up a berm across the front of the property to block road noise. We also used the freebie dirt for filling in low spots in the meadow and the driveway.

If you really aren't sure about what you want and are starting to feel desperately confused, this is a good time to hire a little help. That doesn't mean giving up and letting somebody else design your garden for you. It's simply a question of gathering more specific information from an expert or two. What you need is practical advice, and perhaps some design assistance in the form of suggestions. To find it, look for a garden designer who has done at least a few large projects. Show her—or him—your land and the developing plan, and explain how you want to

*An abrupt cliff edge is buffered with mixed, largely evergreen plantings that retain their beauty and powerful presence in all seasons. The large rock chunks serve both to stabilize the slope and to create planting pockets for shrubs and climbers. Although this planting is just a few years old, already the rocky outcroppings are overgrown enough to appear natural. (Israelit garden, designed by Michael Schultz, Portland, Oregon.)*

*Gravel and paving stones are arranged both to make functional paths and planting areas and to create intriguing shapes when viewed from important locations within the house and garden. Here, when viewed from a large deck, the mixed gravel and river rock suggest a dry riverbed. (Garden designed by Konrad Gauder, Vancouver, Washington.)*

use the area(s) in question. Make notes about the responses you get, then take the resulting ideas back to the design table and massage your map yet again.

If professional advice comes too dear to suit your budget, then hunt around the neighborhood until you find some gardeners. Ask them what they might do in your situation, and be ready to fill a notebook with their responses. You can also use your eyes, noticing how other people in your area have dealt with similar conditions to yours. All this research will leave you much better prepared to oversee the earthworks in your own backyard.

## BUILDING THE HARDSCAPE

Once the soil has been manipulated to your satisfaction, it's time to work on hardscape—paths, patios, terraces, decks, walls and fencing, and water features. These jobs too can be hired out, but most are easy enough for amateurs to tackle if taken on one at a time. If time is of the essence, have the work done for you, for we are all much busier than we think, and few amateur projects are finished on schedule (or under budget). If there is no hurry, consider doing it yourself; it is deeply rewarding to make every part of the garden exactly the way you want it. (Chapter 4, pages 69–74, further explores the installation of walls and fencing; for more information on water features, please see Chapter 3, pg. 42.)

### Constructing Paths

Once any necessary earth reshaping has been accomplished, the next step is to design and install the important access paths into and through the garden. In Chapter 6, we will look at several practical, inexpensive ways to make serviceable paths very quickly, but this is one place where professional assistance can be worth every penny of the extra cost. Paths are vital to the look of a garden: Nothing so quickly pulls an unfocused design into place as a well-made path. They also determine how we use the garden, for the same path that tempts us pleasantly to stroll with friends may leave us struggling along it when pushing a laden garden cart.

Though some kinds of paths are quite easy to make both efficient and attractive, others are more challenging. Should the style of your home and garden demand hard-surfaced paths of brick or stone, then you are very likely to be better off hiring professional help than trying to do this sort of work yourself.

On the other hand, you may be one of those multitalented people who can handle complex, precise, and often difficult jobs very well. If so, you will discover that there are lots of how-to handbooks on making paths, laying brick patios, building decks, and so on, each a small education in itself. Check out several from the library to see which educational style you prefer before buying (the directions in some of these handbooks or series are much clearer and easier to follow than in others). The best such books don't urge us to buy vast quantities of peculiar gadgets with only one function, but stress good-looking projects that are achievable with ordinary tools.

Remember too that hiring help with practical projects doesn't mean your design can't remain personal. There are many excellent craftspeople out there who would be delighted to do the hardscaping for you, on your terms. At the beginning of any large project, optimism often tempts us to take on more than we can really do. When things don't quite work out, pessimism kicks in. We loose heart and decide it's all too much and we can't possibly make a whole garden by ourselves. It's important to realize that we don't all need to do everything, either in the garden or in any other part of our life. The point of garden-making is pleasure, not enslavement to projects that we don't particularly enjoy. Please, please, please, remember to have fun.

### Planting Big Trees

Once the earth has moved and the major hardscape elements have been installed, it's time to bring in any large trees or shrubs. If your garden is encircled by woods or mature landscape of any kind, you may not want to squander your budget on these big plants, which are undeniably expensive. Don't forget, you can borrow your neighbors' trees for nothing, and a small garden without trees of its own may still possess a terrific tree line (the silhouette of the trees against the sky). Indeed, anywhere that green belts and planted buffers are required between houses, there may be enough adjacent greenery that supplementary trees are not necessary. However, in unenclosed new gardens where the tallest plants are hummocky juniper tams smothered in bark chips, the expense of a few good-size trees is more than justified.

It is amazing to see the dramatic difference produced by the introduction of even one mature tree into an empty young garden. This doesn't have to be a huge old thing to work its magic; even a fifteen-footer will give the garden an immediate look of establishment. Where a bare site is encircled (even at a distance) with mature trees, an interesting illusion can be created by adding one or two medium-size trees into the garden. That fringe of tall, bare-trunked older trees near or around the site enforce the impression that native woods have been recently cleared for a new house (as indeed is generally the case). Adding a well-branched, fifteen- or twenty-foot tree makes the site look less raw and makes us feel that the house itself must have been in place for a while for the tree to have achieved its shapely adolescence. The introduction of intermediate trees will similarly give your young garden a look of settled maturity, particularly when you bring in a few adult shrubs as well.

On a small lot, a single sizable tree is enough to work this same minor miracle, especially when there are many mature trees within visual range. Larger lots may require two or three intermediate trees, either grouped or placed singly where they create garden shade and provide visual privacy. If your budget allows, add several groups of three or five good-size shrubs as well, placing them where they help define the garden's perimeters, block unwanted views, and offer backbone support to the new flower borders.

To create the illusion that the garden has been in place for years, combine plants of several sizes. For example, flank one ball-and-burlap tree with two or three ten-gallon shrubs. Supplement these with two or three five-gallon ones, and round the grouping out with a few gallon-size babies. The resulting variety of height is not only more interesting to look at, but recalls the look of natural woodlands, where groups of shrubs and trees are rarely all the same age and size.

Planting oversize trees and shrubs can of course be done by amateurs, but it involves very hard work. The classic rule about digging a ten-dollar hole for a dollar plant still applies here, and few of us are really interested in digging a thousand-dollar hole. Not with a shovel, anyway—but if you had fun with renting the Bobcat for earth moving, you might enjoy doing a little more excavating.

In my first few gardens, it was a point of pride to plant everything myself. Now that my long-abused joints are not so flexible as they were, my personal motto is to hire help for moving—let alone planting—anything bigger than I

*Large trees and shrubs are best planted before the paths and walkways are laid out. The flow of paths within the garden helps determine the shapes and relationships of the plantings beds. (Garden designed by Konrad Gauder, Vancouver, Washington.)*

am. However, those who are young and still in possession of sturdy backs and knees may feel less wimpy about such matters. Should you feel the same way I do, then you may also want to take full advantage of any hired hands (nicely, of course). While you have them around, get those strong young people to plant all the largest trees and shrubs in your landscape.

Though the planting beds may already be laid out, they probably aren't properly prepped. Indeed, they may exist only in the future, their potential sites no more than indicated by stakes and string. Go ahead and plant (or cause to be planted) those big trees and shrubs anyway. The result may well look a bit spotty, like pockets of garden amid the desert. Don't worry about that; the rest of the garden will catch up with the framework in time.

By getting those key trees and shrubs in the ground early, you avoid the inevitable harm caused to smaller plants when larger neighbors are installed late in the game. You also avoid compacting the soil in your carefully prepared beds. However cautious you try to be, it's hard not to

*In smaller spaces, like tiny city lots, it's often better to choose large shrubs to fulfill the role that trees play in larger gardens. Ebullient gardens like this are a welcome gift to the neighborhood and its passersby. (Garden of Lucy Hardiman, Portland, Oregon.)*

cause some damage when trampling through the garden with a hundred-pound tree in your arms.

Siting trees and large shrubs requires significant consideration. This begins not with the selection of which trees you want, but with a thoughtful assessment of how much room you can realistically offer a tree. Keeping their adult height and volume in mind, ask yourself how many trees your yard can really hold. Most yards only have room for one, or at most a handful, even when care is taken to choose trees which remain moderately sized in maturity. Those which will top out between twenty and forty feet are ideal for most suburban gardens.

Before you get your heart set on having any one particular type of tree, figure out what size your garden's potential tree(s) should be, both now and in the future. You save a lot of heartache and expense by thinking these things through before planting. To help make up your mind, get a good reference book on trees (*The Year in Trees*, by J. C. Ralston and Kim Tripp, Timber Press, 1995, is outstanding). Next, visit some parks or your local arboretum to see how your candidates will look when they grow up. Ultimate height is important, but so is width. How far will the crown of that tree spread? Will it soon cast far more shade more than you want it to? Other qualities to consider are detailed in Chapter 6, but for now, these few will keep you busy enough.

The same considerations go for those large shrubs. Will they quickly block a window view you want to frame, requiring more frequent pruning than you care to commit to? Do they get tubby in middle age, spreading inexorably over the pathway? If you need to hack them back often, will they lose their will to regenerate? Will they grow leggy and scraggly when shaded out by that presently small tree which will soon be much taller? Don't allow yourself to buy any of these critically important plants on impulse. You might get lucky and make a perfect match between situation and plant, but it isn't a sure thing. Until you become comfortably familiar with the important qualities and characteristics of a number of woody plants, don't guess.

It isn't just a question of accidentally picking a dud. Though there are very few "bad plants," many terrific ones can become monsters in the wrong situation. To guide your selection toward plants that will do what you want them to over time, read the chapter on the selection of trees and shrubs before making your final choices.

SIX

# PRACTICAL PATHS

## Simple, Handsome Paths to Make in a Weekend

*Though the most formal kinds of paving are best left to professionals, even those of us who are not especially dexterous can create useful and attractive paths in very* short order. Personally, I am not all that handy when it comes to masonry, and prefer to let experts do any work that involves heavy substances like concrete and stones. In my own garden, I use the easily made garden paths which are explained here in detail.

Naturally, these quickie paths don't hold up for years, as good brick or concrete work will. Most need periodic grooming or replenishing to maintain their looks. Some need sturdy edgers to keep the path materials from spilling into garden beds (or vice versa). None are as smooth underfoot as harder

*English cottage gardens often feature paths made from irregularly shaped and sized stones set in a patchwork pattern called crazy paving. If the pavers are widely spaced, they are frequently interplanted with running herbs such as creeping thymes or Corsican mint. Where plants with more variation in height are planted into crazy paving, it's best to use larger pavers to avoid creating slippery or unsafe footing. (Garden of Elaine and Dave Whitehead, Saanich, British Columbia.)*

surfaces, making them slightly less convenient to use in terms of loaded wheelbarrows.

Their advantages are that they are quick and simple to make, with instant and powerful landscaping effect. Laid out with care, these paths are handsome and fairly lasting. Best of all, they are cheap, especially when compared with the price of careful brick or stone work. For those who move often, these quickie paths make real sense.

## TURF PATHS

Easiest of all is the turf path. When you are creating new beds on top of lawn, making a grassy pathway is child's play. Order in your topsoil, have it dumped where you want it, then smooth it out to make instant planting beds as detailed in Chapter 1. If the grass beneath them is rough meadow, you may find that a few persistent weeds such as creeping buttercup or horsetails will need pulling for a season or two. However, a depth of eight to twelve inches of soil topped with mulch is enough to smother almost anything beneath it.

To keep the grass paths clear, slope back the planting bed soil in a gradual rather than an abrupt edge. Mulch the beds deeply (I use four to six inches of composted dairy manure), keep your paths tightly mown, and you will have very little problem with weeds roaming into the beds. An occasional touch-up with a half-moon edging tool keeps the lawn line looking trim. If you prefer, leave a narrow (one- or two-inch) gap at each path edge for the mower wheel, and you will only need to hand trim once in a while.

## MULCH PATHS

If you want a softer look, with plants spilling into the path, forget grass. The tight mowing needed to keep the grass in control precludes the tumbling perennials that mellow the sharp edge of the bed. They are invariably injured by the mower, and a great deal of handwork is necessary to keep the underlying grass tidy. What's more, that grass is soon browned off, leaving dead patches which look awful for more than half the year.

Consider instead a mulch path. These are ideal between raised beds, where the gentle slope of the planting soil makes a natural boundary for a path. The mulch material can be anything you can get a good supply of, but the result will be far less confusing to children and visitors if you use different-looking mulches on paths and beds. For instance, if you have golden brown washed dairy manure on the beds, deep brown shredded bark

*Shredded bark, wood shavings, or wood chips all make an excellent path surface. Attractively colored even when fresh, wood materials age with grace, turning soft grays and warm browns in maturity. Forgiving underfoot, they provide safe walking when wet or dry. Organic materials such as hazel-nut hulls, coffee chaff, and crushed peanut shells have similar attributes and may be available free for the hauling. (Garden of Ernie and Marietta O'Byrne, Eugene, Oregon.)*

*Gravel paths drain quickly and they provide safe passage when rain slickens rock and brick. Round pea gravel can be treacherous and slippery, but medium-fine crushed rock (the size called 3/4–minus) compacts well and won't roll underfoot. (Chase garden, Orting, Washington.)*

or sand-colored wood shavings will make the paths obvious even to pets.

Crushed gravel and shredded bark are common path materials, and both are quite attractive, but neither feel pleasant to naked feet. Wood shavings feel softer underfoot and are splinterless. Peanut hulls, sawdust, and wheat straw are other good choices. Any locally available material should be considered.

## Cloth Liners

To keep weeds down, cover the path with horticultural barrier cloth before heaping on mulch. This woven plastic cloth is slowly degradable, but lasts for many years. The tight weave allows water and air to pass freely through its mesh, but blocks weeds and (usually) root-disturbing critters like moles as well. Sold at most nurseries and garden centers, barrier cloth comes in various widths, from three to forty feet or more. Buy a size wider than the path you want to make, so the edges can be extended under the planting beds. (Otherwise they have a bad habit of emerging through the mulch, no matter how deeply you layer it.)

Buy a box of cloth pins or anchors as well—these look like a cross between tent stakes and giant staples. Their sharp ends penetrate barrier cloth when the flat tops are tapped with a hammer. Pushed flush with the ground, they keep the cloth from wrinkling or shifting beneath the mulch. Next, smoothly slope the planting bed soil over those extra inches on each side of the path. This will firmly anchor the cloth, and you won't be bothered by unsightly edges.

### Newsprint Liners

If your budget is tight, you can substitute old newspapers for the horticultural barrier cloth. Years ago, colored printing ink often had traces of lead and other heavy metals that made newspaper mulch unsuitable for vegetable garden paths. (The concern was that these poisonous metals would leach out of the newspapers into the soil and contaminate the vegetables—not a good idea.) These days, however, newspaper inks are almost exclusively soy- or vegetable-based. When in doubt, call your local paper to find out what kind of inks they use. If nobody seems to know (unusual in this eco-conscious age), avoid using color supplements, which were the culprits in the past.

Unless you have accumulated a lifetime supply of old papers or can raid a nearby recycling center, newspaper liners are most practical with shorter, narrow paths. For one thing, you must layer the papers thickly or they become all but worthless as weed barriers in very short order. A thickness of ten or twelve sheets is a minimum for small paths, but more is definitely better. If you can muster so much paper, a thickness of two to three inches is not too deep. Though folded paper compresses over time, it cushions the feet nicely, even when covered with sawdust or shredded bark.

Newspaper paths tend to break down around the edges, leaving thin spots where weeds can penetrate with relative ease. To avoid this, use extra-thick folded papers along path edges, lining them up to overlap generously with the adjacent sections. As with barrier cloth, make newspaper path liners at least a foot wider than the intended path. Disguise the edges as you would with barrier cloth, and there will be very few weed problems. Whichever you use, once it is securely in place, cover it with several inches of your chosen mulching material.

### Straw Mulch

Where work paths are temporary and will later be incorporated into large planting beds, straw mulch is an excellent choice, and not just short term. Though this material seems best suited to informal settings, it can look surprisingly handsome. Lay out the straw with care and it takes on a Japanesque elegance that works even in formal settings.

If such paths are to be used for only a few seasons, you won't need to put down any kind of barrier cloth or paper. You may get a little weed penetration along the edges, but thick layers of

straw (six to twelve inches) keep the underlying soil so moist and soft that any stray weeds will be very easy to pull. When the time comes to make the path disappear, just pull any loose straw aside, then top off the depression where the path ran with topsoil. There may be some compacted straw mashed into the bottom layer, but that's no problem. Heap soil over it, tuck that loose straw between backbone shrubs, and mulch the new bed to match its surroundings.

### Laying Out and Leveling Mulched Paths

No matter which kind of garden path you decide on, there is a small amount of general preparation work to be done before laying on your mulching substance of choice. Because mulched paths are heaped with soft or shifting materials, it isn't crucial to make the pathways perfectly level, as they must be for laid flagstones or patterned bricks. It is, however, worth taking the time to make any path relatively smooth right from the beginning, for flaws have an annoying way of asserting themselves later.

To do this, remove any large protruding rocks or root stumps and cut away big bumps of compacted soil with a flat shovel. Next, rake the whole pathway with a heavy metal rake (the straight, flat kind that looks like a bent comb, not the spreading fan rakes used for gathering leaves or grass clippings). Fill in any low spots with soil and get

*An ordinary entryway path is made personal by a charming pebble mosaic created from smooth beach stones. Stones, tiles, shells, and similarly decorative materials can be fused to concrete walkways and steps with hard-wearing marine epoxy. The same substance can be mixed with coarse builder's sand and painted over concrete paths that were given a slick, overly slippery finish to add better traction. (Garden of Nani Wadoops and Ron Wagoner, Portland, Oregon.)*

*Neat brickwork looks best near formally designed houses, and large slabs of stone look most at home with informal styles such as farmhouses. Here, a handsome mixture of brickwork and paving makes a striking transition between the formal seating area near the house and a walkway leading to a wilder part of the garden. (Garden designed by Pamela Burton, Santa Monica, California.)*

the kids to trample on them until the new soil is compacted and feels as hard as the surrounding dirt. Rake it out again, then lay out and peg down a layer of horticultural barrier cloth (or newspapers). Now you can surface your lovely new path with whatever mulch you have chosen.

When you are working with a new yard that has not been planted or sodded at all, such raking is a great way to play around with ideas about where you might want your various paths and beds to run. It's easy to describe soft lines and sinuous curves or lay them out arrow straight, if that's what best suits your site. Where sod has already been laid down use a pair of flexible garden hoses to mark the flow of any proposed paths; it's much easier than staking out paths with sticks and string, a traditional method that only works well for marking straight lines. The stick-and-string method is also dangerous to the health of those who like to wander the growing garden at night. If you trip over a hose, no harm is done. Tumble over a string and you bring the whole bothersome business down with you, usually getting a stick in the eye or some tender portion of your anatomy during the excitement.

### Laying out Planting Beds and Borders

This hose trick also works for laying out freeform planting beds. You can fasten several hoses together to make really big beds or longer paths. When you get your lines just right, it is a breeze to replicate them accurately by replacing the hoses a few feet at a time using wooden bender board or soft plastic edging strips.

If you want to try out alternative routes or placement, mark the original lines with horticultural lime before shifting the hoses. You can sometimes find inexpensive rolling lawn markers (they look like a revolving spaceship on a stick)

*Large concrete pavers can look industrial or parklike rather than gardenly. To make them blend into the garden setting, the designer disguises their hard edges with spilling plants and casual clusters of ornamental pots. Wide benches and deep borders help keep the generous proportions in balance as well. (Garden designed by Dan Borroff, Tacoma, Washington.)*

*Pavers set into sand are subject to frost heaves in cold climates. To avoid such problems, pavers can be set into concrete. These smooth and fairly flat stones make good footing, especially as the concrete is coarsely textured. (Garden of Robin Hopper and Judi Dyelle, Metchosin, British Columbia.)*

that sift out small amounts of lime. If your hardware store doesn't have one, check out sporting goods stores, where they are sometimes sold for marking out badminton or lawn tennis courts.

Even if you aren't a sports fan, these little lawn markers are very useful during the planning stages. Some people use them as planting guides as well, marking out sections of large borders with swoops and swirls. In England, they are sometimes used to transfer a garden design from paper to border. The plantings beds are gridded out with sticks and string to correlate to the grid of the graph paper. The planting patterns are enlarged and copied directly onto the soil, using thin lines of lime (or sometimes powdered chalk) to guide the gardeners. This is an awful lot of work, but the method has enormous appeal for those who like to be very precise in everything they do.

However, this has never worked for me, because I have never seen the paper garden that correlates so exactly to the actual one. For most of us, the design process is an invaluable aid, but the actual laying out of paths and planting areas will be somewhat different in real life than it is on paper. Paper gardens are always perfect, but real ones are rarely so cooperative. When your ideal plans are altered by unforseen circumstances, remember that this is not a bad reflection on your planning skills. It's just another instance of restless, woolly life intruding abruptly on our dreams. Though the awakening can be rude, the result is usually salutary for us and our gardens.

SEVEN

# DIRT WORK

## How's Your Dirt? Testing, Amending, and Building Your Soil

*At last, it's time for some practical applications of all the pondering and measuring you have done. Through the process of finding the paths and resting places in your* garden, you have also figured out where and how big the planting beds will be. That's one of the payoffs from following the sometimes complex design procedures outlined in previous chapters.

*Great gardens start with great soil. To transform common dirt into splendid soil, amend often with tilth builders such as compost and aged manures. Good tilth creates soil conditions that promote healthy root growth. Well-rooted plants are happy plants that perform unstintingly over a long season. (Garden of Ernie and Marietta O'Byrne, Eugene, Oregon.)*

Assembling your garden map and charting the physical characteristics of your chosen garden site undeniably takes a lot of time, but it is genuinely worth the extra effort. It's easy to get restless and want to skip the preliminaries in favor of immediate action.

We start buying armloads of plants, then realize we need shovels and trowels. That's enough, though, right? What does it take to make a plant happy? Dirt and water, anybody knows that. Soil preparation? Dirt work? What does that mean? Dirt's dirt, right?

Well, yes and no. You might get incredibly lucky and begin your gardening experience with pure sandy loam, the stuff of the gods. If so, you can grow anything you want with ease and you won't need a book to tell you how. Please don't think, however, that I'm curmudgeonly for mentioning that the odds of this happening are not great. Fortunately, just by making a few simple observations, you can save yourself a lot of trouble and needless expense.

Most of your information-gathering can be done right away. A few observations will have to wait for events like a big rain, but you can also fudge a bit (by spraying the ground with a hose, for example) to learn or figure out what you need to know. The idea here is to assess exactly what it is you've got to offer your prospective plants. Then, instead of suffering through expensive trial and error (and error and error and error) plantings, you will be able to succeed with a higher percentage of plants, because you can select those that are able to adapt to your conditions.

To get there, we need to determine just exactly what those conditions are. As we have seen, many important aspects of garden design involve the big picture. Now, smaller details need recording as well. For instance, without fairly accurate measurements about the dimensions of each proposed planting bed, few people are able to estimate the right number of plants needed to fill them.

It is also vitally important to understand your site's microclimates and moisture zones. Locate and mark any areas that are open to wind, or always sunny. Look, too, for places that are constantly moist, or root-saturated, dust-dry spots such as we find beneath big old cedars or beech trees.

*Every garden boasts microclimates, areas which are markedly drier or wetter, sunnier or shadier than others. By clustering sun lovers on warm, sunny steps, they can thrive even in a cool, relatively shady garden. Bog lovers can be placed in soggy spots, and desert dwellers are offered spots along the driveway, where reflected heat and light will make them feel right at home. (Madrona Garden, designed by Michael Schultz, Portland, Oregon.)*

Such places are never impossible to plant, but even with soil replenishment, they will only succeed as garden beds long term if the right plants are put there. While few common border plants will grow in these spots without considerable help, species that live with similar conditions in the wild are also excellent candidates in the garden. For instance, where root competition and drought present difficulties for pampered border plants, native bleeding hearts (*Dicentra* species) and ferns will often thrive.

A garden's wet spots may be permanent or seasonal. During a recent downpour, while we were transferring wet groceries into my tiny car in the middle of a giant, semipermanent puddle, a fellow gardener at the grocery store reminded me that it's a great idea to look at the garden during (or just after) a heavy rain.

This is what you are looking for: Are there places where the water pools quickly? Places where rain water stands for hours or even days after the rain? Mark these, with indications of how long the water rests in each spot. Persistent wet spots usually indicate compacted soil, hardpan, or other problems. (For example, in one garden I had, standing water indicated a hidden, long-buried driveway.)

After identifying potentially challenging areas, we can decide how to deal with them. A poor planting site might be a terrific spot for a patio, potting shed or compost heap. How about the dog run or the kids' sand box? Any of these would be far more rewarding to live with than a soggy bed of sad plants.

## SOIL TESTING: HOW'S THAT TILTH?

It's also well worth figuring out where your garden's best soil is, so your plan can take advantage of it. If you have been gardening for a while, you can probably tell what kind of soil you have where just by poking about with a shovel. If you are newer to gardening, you will have to conduct a few informal tests to find out.

*These large mixed borders are sited on a sloping hillside on heavy clay soil that prevents proper drainage. Many plants would drown in the soggy soil during the long, wet winter unless the soil were well amended. Yearly applications of manure and compost (spread in spring and fall) keep the combined communities of shrubs, perennials, bulbs, and ground covers in top condition, as evidenced by the following photograph. (The Northwest Perennial Alliance Border at the Bellevue Botanic Garden, Bellevue, Washington.)*

First, take a handful of soil and squeeze it. If the soil compacts into a tight ball, you have clay. If it pours out of your hand, you have sand. If it forms a loose ball, but crumbles freely, your luck is in; you have a nice sandy loam, which most plants prefer.

A further test involves drainage, and should be performed wherever you plan to install beds and borders. In each spot, dig a hole about a foot deep and fill it with water. If the water drains away as fast as you can pour it (or within about half an hour), your soil is sandy, and you will need to add all the humus (see below) you can muster. If the water is still there hours later, or lingers into the next day (or next week), you have clay soil, and should consider making raised beds to avoid root rot. Adding significant amounts of coarse builder's sand or road grit to your soil mix will also help. Clay soils hold moisture and nutrients well, but they tend to be hard on plant roots, which need fresh air as well.

In good sandy loam, the water will drain away over an hour or two, leaving your plants refreshed but able to breathe. This means you can provide good conditions for a wide range of plants, and won't have to make raised beds unless you want to for design purposes.

## Soil pH: Sweet and Sour Soils

If I devote a lot of time to talking about dirt, well, there's a good reason for this fixation. Dirt is the foundation on which the garden is made. The best design in the world can't be realized on lousy dirt. Good soil, on the other hand, can support an incredible variety of plants. Healthy plants, in turn, make even a simple design look great.

One of the best ways to grow happy, healthy plants is by making sure their soil isn't too sweet or too sour. Where I live in the Northwest, the main types of native soils are either loose and sandy or heavy clay. In either case, their condition is further defined by acid-base balance, or pH. West of the Cascade Mountains, our dirt is very likely to be acid (below 7 in pH). East of the mountains, most soils are alkaline (above 7). In a few favored places, the soil is neutral—a perfect 7. This may not be a great score in the Olympic games, but anywhere near our own Olympic Mountains (the second biggest range in the Northwest), it's a definite winner.

You don't have to be a chemist to be a good gardener, but a basic understanding of soil chemistry will definitely help. In technical terms, pH has to do with the relative balance of hydrogen and hydroxyl on a scale from zero to fourteen. A higher percentage of hydrogen in soil (or water, or anything else) indicates acidity; an excess of hydroxyl indicates alkalinity.

When the two are in balance, the substance is considered neutral. When they aren't, each successive pH level is ten times greater than the last one. This means a soil with a pH of 5 is ten times more acid than one of 6 and a hundred times more acid than one of 7.

Relax; the worst of the techno-talk is over. In garden terms, the terminology is pretty simple. Neutral soils are called sweet, while acid ones are considered sour. This sounds bad, but all you

### TESTING THE pH FOR PICKY PLANTS

Lots of vegetables and a number of ornamentals will grow better in improved soils than in strongly acid or alkaline ones. If you have been disappointed in the performance of your vegetables or flowers, despite giving them the best care you can, pH might be the problem.

To find out, have your soil tested. If you prefer, you can do it yourself with a simple kit sold at most nurseries. The kits are not quite as accurate as commercial testing services, but most are good enough to pinpoint a problem. Most states also offer soil tests, usually at a modest cost, through the county extension service. (They also offer a host of useful garden advice and information for free.) You can get the extension service telephone number at your local library, if you can't find it in the phone book.

have to do is look around to see that many so-called sour soils can support an exceptional abundance of native flora, not to mention thousands of garden plants.

### *Neutralizing Your Soil*

While plants are pretty adaptable, most grow best in a fairly narrow pH range (between 6 and 6.8). However, soil testing out between about 6 and 8 won't need adjusting except for picky plants like blueberries, rhododendrons, and azaleas, which insist upon acid soils. Soil amendments such as agricultural lime can be added to reduce the acidity of native soils. (Never use industrial or slaked lime; that's for outhouses.) If your garden soil is pronouncedly acid or alkaline, though, it makes more sense to take advantage of those natural inclinations. Instead of trying to amend your whole garden, find out which native and exotic plants enjoy your local conditions and concentrate on growing those. In most cases, you will have a very large selection to chose from, and instead of sulking, those plants will appreciate your soil just as it is.

## Getting the Lead Out

If your new garden surrounds an elderly house and you plan to grow edibles of any kind, you will need to have one more test done, either through the extension service or a private testing lab. Anywhere you intend to grow edibles, fruit trees, vegetables, or even flowers that might end up in salads or on cakes, it is very important to have the soil in those areas checked for lead contamination.

This can be caused by lead-based paint flaking off an older house, but may also exist where painted fences—which may have disappeared without a visible trace—once stood. Lead from car exhaust is also a hazard in urban and suburban roadside gardens, where it may persist in the soil long after lead-free gasoline has gained general usage.

It's a good idea to have the soil checked in the children's play yard as well, since youngsters are especially vulnerable to lead poisoning. If lead is present, you can choose either to remove the polluted dirt or to cover it with barrier cloth (as discussed in the Chapter 6). You can then bring in fresh topsoil and turf the area.

You could also cover the trouble spot with six or more inches of ground-up recycled rubber tires. This makes a bouncy, splinter-free surface that can handle tricycles and wagons with ease. It won't stain clothing, and cuts down remarkably on bumps and bruises from falling off swing sets and so forth. Many urban recycling centers can supply this stuff, which seems to have a different proprietary name in every city.

Another fine material called Softstep™ has similar properties, but is made of recycled wood fiber. (To find a source near you, call 1-800-422-0603.) If you have trouble locating these materials, contact a local landscape architect who designs schools and playgrounds for advice on where to buy something similar in your area.

## MAKE BEAUTIFUL DIRT

As experienced garden-makers know well, good soil is at least as important as the plants it supports. You may notice that, generous though they may be with plants that reproduce themselves freely, few of our gardening friends are quite as openhanded with good dirt. Indeed, it is polite practice to bring a bag or two of your own soil, as well as extra pots and flats, when divisions of plants are offered.

Showing up empty-handed and expecting to be given access to the compost heap or potting shed is tolerated in the new gardener, who is presumed not to know any better. However, if an experienced gardener does this, it is considered poor form.

This isn't because gardeners are stingy—far from it. It's just that, for many of us, dirt work becomes very personal. For one thing, it can take years to turn sullen clay or sifting sand into rich, fluffy soil. Only frequent amendment with every good source of humus we can muster makes lovely garden dirt out of many native soils.

I still recall with a pang of loss the soil I left behind when we moved from Seattle over ten years ago. After years of tending, that stiff, unforgiving clay had grown so open that I could plunge my arm in it up to my elbow. When we left, the back garden was soon covered by a deck and I wished I had taken the dirt as well as most of my plants.

For one thing, my new garden had wretched soil that needed lots of improvement before we could even begin to plant. Not only that, but I had also left my compost heap behind. Like good soil, a large stash of homemade compost is worth more than rubies when the planting of a new garden begins. Dozens, even hundreds of plants are waiting to be installed in their new homes, and the better their start, the better they will grow. Plant or pot them up in compost and good soil and most plants will leap eagerly into active life. Shove them higgledy-piggledy into unprepared ground and they are likely to languish instead.

In many new gardens, the earth is scraped to hardpan during the house construction process. Generally, topsoil has been spread (quite thinly) over this impermeable surface wherever the contractor assumes you will want your beds to be. Hardpan, however, boasts no worms, and few commercial topsoils offer any worm-life either. Without worms to do the mixing for us, the new soil won't blend into the old, but remains layered like chocolate icing on a sand-colored cake.

In older gardens, the situation is different but the results are similar. Tired-out soils that have nurtured lawns for many years without much care in return are often nearly sterile.

Even when commercial feeds have been used, their results are only temporary. Because most fertilizers don't improve the soil, it remains impoverished. As soon as that quickie nitrogen boost has been absorbed by your lawn, the goodness is gone.

Soil exhaustion can be treated in the same ways that we improve hardpan or other impoverished soils, but whatever the difficulty you face, anybody gardening on inhospitable soil needs to address the situation before planting anything at all. After so much planning, it's highly tempting to plunge into planting and simply hope for the best. Be assured, the best will certainly not happen without significant help from us.

Spring and fall are the optimum times to plant a new garden, but not the best time to build new beds. The wise gardener will spend any intervening time in improving the planting areas to be ready for prime time. If you end up needing to make new beds in spring or fall, a few caveats will help you avoid several common mistakes that can hamper your garden's future growth and development.

During spring and fall, seasonal rains make even droughty soils moist. Barren clay soils look dark and rich, while light ones appear warmly golden. Autumn planters won't notice anything wrong immediately, but as soon as summer arrives this deception will pass: The clay will regress to adobe and the sand will return to its desert state.

Both kinds of soil need to be well and truly amended before becoming a happy medium for plant growth. In both cases, humus is the first ingredient to supply. In garden terms, humus is the stuff of life, the organic material that turns inert mineral particles into living soil.

### Feeding Soil First

Most gardeners are aware that humus is important for good root development, but aren't so sure about why. When you really understand how humus content affects plant performance, soil building gets a lot more satisfying. Indeed, for practiced gardeners, it becomes an art form. Creating gourmet soils and watching plants respond to them so positively is one of the most exciting parts of garden making.

To make great dirt, we need to know what our plants require. Plants eat dirt, and a proper balance of nutrients is as important to their well-being as it is to ours. Basic soil components—nitrogen, potassium, and phosphorus—are like proteins, fats, and carbohydrates, while trace elements are the equivalent of vitamin and mineral supplements. Humus acts like insulin, making nutritional elements available to plants just as insulin allows our bodies to access the food we eat.

A well-balanced soil mix will meet the needs of a large majority of garden plants. A few plants have special needs that demand specific alterations in diet. In every case, deficiencies in

*High summer fills the borders to the bursting point, but the show doesn't stop until the last flickers of fall have burned to ash. Overly rich feeds would promote excess growth that could quickly lead to overcrowding and disease, but slow, continual feeds (such as organic supplements) keep the plantings in good health and balance. (The Northwest Perennial Alliance Border at the Bellevue Botanic Garden, Bellevue, Washington.)*

any significant nutrients (especially the big three) can cause health problems. Since most native soils are imbalanced or deficient to some degree, many plants never get the chance to perform optimally. The good news is that nearly all plant problems, including pest attacks and many diseases, can be prevented or cured through proper nutrition. The place to start is at ground level.

In my new yard, I found a sad little dusty miller plant trying to grow beneath the overhanging limbs of a fir tree. Dusty miller is a tough plant. Its felted, silvery leaves are designed to conserve moisture, making it able to withstand drought very well. This is good, because that poor plant was set where it couldn't get a drop of natural water.

What's more, it had clearly been planted straight into the native soil, with no attempt at all to open or improve the tight clay. Though the plant had been in the ground for at least a few years, it had not grown or produced new foliage at all. When I dug it up, you could still see the original rootball, exactly the same size and shape as an ordinary four-inch pot. The soil it had been placed in was so stiff and solid that those poor roots couldn't even begin to penetrate through it.

Had the dirt been better, the lack of water wouldn't have mattered. That dusty miller would have been five times its beginning size, simply because its roots would have stretched deeper and found the water it needed. Healthy, beautiful dirt makes it a lot easier for our plants to fend for themselves.

I first realized the importance of making beautiful dirt years ago when I grew mostly vegetables. To see if it really mattered, I amended half the garden beds thoroughly. The others were loosened and smoothed but not improved. Sure enough, the amended beds outproduced the others significantly.

What's more, plants in the amended beds grew bigger and had far fewer pests. It seemed weird to see one patch of broccoli crawling with bugs while the other a few feet away remained almost untouched. At season's end, when I turned the soil, I noticed that root growth in the amended beds was extensive. In the other beds, many of the plants were like that dusty miller, having barely outgrown their original rootball. The key difference was the humus content of the beds.

*Good Humus Makes Good Gardens*

Humus is the Wonder Bread of soil building, functioning in many important ways. Humus is almost as squishy, too. Indeed, just as its amazing compressibility makes Wonder Bread the savvy kid's spitball material of choice, humus gives non-clay-based soils cling, the capacity to hold a shape. This pleasant textural quality, also called tilth, is what experienced gardeners are looking for when they pick up and squeeze a handful of dirt.

Humus is organic plant food, but organic in the original sense: the carbon-based leftovers from both animal and vegetable life forms. Mostly, it comes from decaying vegetation. The materials that are commonly called humus are really its precursors: sawdust and manures, grass clippings and chopped hay, leaves and shredded bark are all potential humus, because as they decompose, that's what they become.

As they rot, the breakdown process floods the soil with raw nutrients. Before plants can use these nutrients, they need to be further processed by soil microbes, just as our food is broken down into nutritional building blocks through digestion.

The living bacteria and microbes that perform this service also eat humus, but need different bits of it than the plants do. Just as trees take up carbon dioxide and give off oxygen at night, soil biota and plants have evolved a mutually beneficial digestive relationship with humus (and with hummus as well, should you toss any leftover chickpeas in the compost heap).

*The Living Sponge*

Besides feeding the soil, humus also holds an exceptional amount of water, acting as a living sponge. Tired, humus-poor soil can only take up relatively minor amounts of water; about 20 percent of the soil's own dry weight is a typical carrying capacity for unimproved urban or suburban dirt. In contrast, woodland duff, the deep soil found in undisturbed woods, can absorb and hold up to 500 percent of its own weight in water.

Forest duff may consist of centuries' worth of decomposed leaves and whatnot, but even a quickly made garden compost can retain a volume of water weighing 300 to 400 percent of its dry weight. Given the average plant's need for a consistent supply of moisture, having a lot of humus in the soil makes good sense.

In order to do its work well, however, humus needs to be applied in quantity. To be fully effective, we need to incorporate enough humus to equal between one quarter to one half the total volume of soil in each bed or border to be amended.

How much humus you need for optimal improvement depends on the soil you start off with. Dry, sandy soil, or dusty, compacted, and impoverished soil can use half again as much humus by volume. Open, well-textured soils that drain nicely yet hold together in a loose, crumbly ball need a lesser amount. Remember, too, that these are ballpark measurements; making good soil isn't like making a soufflé, where miscalculating an ingredient can spell disaster. In most soils, adding practically any organic tilth amendment (humus builder) in almost any quantity will make a positive difference.

### Acquiring, Storing, and Applying Garden Humus

Compost is widely touted as the soil builder of choice. Homemade compost has many advantages, especially when you recycle a large variety of plant material through the heap. (See Chapter 8, pages 131–135, for detailed instructions on making homemade compost.) Since there are literally thousands of kinds of soil biota, each preferring slightly different combinations of nutrients, the broader the mix we feed them, the healthier they are. Soil full of healthy bacteria makes for healthy plants.

In a brand-new garden, however, mature compost is a rare luxury. Until your own compost is ready to use in quantity, you can use humus builders like manure, sawdust, and shredded bark. In many parts of the country, good sources of garden humus abound and are often free for the taking. When neighbors tidy yards or

*These lushly planted borders are mulched each year with generous quantities of aged dairy manure. Short stakes mark the resting crowns of perennials or bulbs that might be smothered by an overdose of mulch. (The Northwest Perennial Alliance Border at the Bellevue Botanic Garden, Bellevue, Washington.)*

abundant and continual supply of resources produced by their pets.

Sometimes you can even get the stuff delivered. Many lawn and yard care services are happy to bring biodegradable plant materials right to your compost area. The crews that trim trees under power lines are also glad to have a nearby spot for dumping the shredded chips.

Many small food businesses generate a goodly supply of humus. Here in the Northwest, local vintners and microbrewers allow gardeners to take home grape must and spent hops for free. Both make excellent compost when mixed well with grass clippings and shredded leaves. A nearby peanut-butter factory supplies endless quantities of peanut hulls, which can be used for compost or to surface paths. Chocolate makers have cocoa bean hulls to spare, and specialty coffee roasters

communities groom parks and school grounds, large quantities of fallen leaves and grass clippings are often available.

In suburbs and rural areas, riding stables and small dairy farms often have extra manure and stall sweepings to give away. Private owners of horses, goats, sheep, rabbits, and cows are generally quite pleased to have help using up the

*By late spring, these same borders are filling fast. The mulch no longer looks obtrusive, and spring bloomers have already begun to feast on the nutrients. (The Northwest Perennial Alliance Border at the Bellevue Botanic Garden, Bellevue, Washington.)*

sometimes burn a batch of beans. (These make truly gorgeous paths.)

You can also stop by the nearest coffee bar or latte stand (not during rush hour, of course) and ask what they do with those big tubs of coffee grounds. If you volunteer to take the stuff away on a regular basis, your offer will probably be gratefully accepted. The same goes for places where vegetables or cut flowers are prepared for market; the scraps and leftovers can be recycled through the compost.

While vegetable and flower scraps make splendid compost, mixed food scraps can present problems. Health department regulations often prohibit schools or restaurants from allowing anybody to use leftovers, even for composting purposes. One exception is the produce department of grocery stores, which sometimes have whole cases of lost lettuces or rotten radishes to discard.

In any case, food scraps need careful composting. Fatty scraps like cheese, milk products, or meat, will attract dogs, rats, raccoons, and other scavengers. Not only will they disturb your compost pile (and your garden), but they can add undesirable elements to it. Not all animal manures are good composters, and some have nasty viral components (as witness the fatal New Mexican hanta virus, carried by mice).

Good humus can also come from recycled paper products. Find an office where paper is routinely shredded and offer to remove their supplies regularly. Nearly all black and white copy is garden safe, though materials like film or Mylar are not. Shredded newsprint is a fine compost addition, and most papers now use soy-based inks exclusively, so even the colored supplements are all right to use. To be sure, call the paper and ask what kind of inks they use. If the colored inks are not soy-based, don't recycle the funnies through the garden.

Old wallboard can also be recycled, though it's not very scenic. The crumbly white stuff inside it is gypsum, which helps to open up tight clays. The slow way to recycle wallboard is to dump it on the compost pile and let the rain (and time) break it down. Shredding the stuff works best of all, but wallboard will clog conventional shredders and dull the blades. Happily, a machete or large garden knife makes a great shredding tool, and the work is quite therapeutic.

The one factor you need to consider in regard to soliciting free composting materials is follow-through. When gardeners ask for coffee grounds or vegetable scraps, we need to be responsible about collection of those materials. For a small business, it can be more trouble than it's worth to have somebody take away scraps just now and then. To make it worth their time, band together with a few gardening friends and form a humus collection coop. That way, good material gets reliably recycled, the businesses don't have to pay to dispose of their biodegradable wastes, and many gardens can benefit.

Most of these humus builders need to age and mellow before being added to the garden. During the warm season, you can simply add them to the compost heap, making new piles (or filling new bins) as needed. If you amass large quantities in winter, find a corner of the garden where a heap of decomposing material won't be a problem. Cover each heap with a tarp so winter rains can't leach the nutrients out. (Why doesn't some clever manufacturer make tasteful, Monet-blue tarps, instead of that incredibly obtrusive electric blue . . . now there's a market niche!)

Leaching is problematic in nonwinter months too: In heavy rains there is a likelihood of seepage into streams and storm drains. Manure runoff in particular poses a significant health hazard, and must be properly contained. To prevent inadvertent pollution, surround storage piles with hay bales. Once the hay is saturated with runoff, replace it, using the soggy stuff for mulch or the compost pile.

If a manure pile is on or near a slope, you can further protect water supplies by adding silt fences to the hay bales. Used to keep construction site runoff out of the water supply, silt fences are made of a mesh that captures fine particles.

Also, it is wise to wear gloves when you handle manures, since open wounds can become infected through contact. This is especially true of fresh or incompletely composted manures which aren't garden ready. This holds for peat moss too, which can also cause dangerous respiratory infections, so use a respirator whenever you handle it. Indeed, peat moss is no longer a recommended garden additive, both because of serious health problems and because it is approaching endangered status. The peat bogs that have been harvested for garden use took millennia to form. Once the peat is gone, the bogs require several thousand years to recover.

### Balancing Humus and Nitrogen

Where wood by-products like sawdust and shredded bark abound, they often constitute a large proportion of the compost mix. They can be great tilth makers, but it's important to be aware that wood-based humus builders use a lot of nitrogen in the breakdown process. Unless you supply more, the end result will be a fluffy, humus-rich soil that is nitrogen poor. Good sources of supplemental nitrogen are the seed meals—cottonseed, soy, and so forth. Ammonium sulfate also works fine, and is easy to find in most nurseries.

You can mix nitrogen directly into the composting materials, but it isn't easy to blend them well. I find it simpler to apply the supplementary nitrogen when you add humus builders to garden soil. To do this, mark the beds off in ten-by-ten foot grids or the equivalent (one hundred square feet). Spread out your humus builder on top (the manure or whatever), then measure its depth. In most cases, you will have between four and six inches, but with really poor soil, you could end up using close to a foot of amendment. Next, cover each marked (hundred-foot-square) area with a pound of nitrogen for every inch of humus builder.

Oh that math! Many of you might want to shut the book and take a walk at this point, wondering what this has to do with gardening. Really, it's not that bad: Let's say you used six inches of sawdust. You need six pounds of nitrogen for each hundred-square-foot bed. And remember, if you are using compost or aged manure, you don't need any extra nitrogen unless your soil test showed a deficiency.

Now, mix and mingle the whole business into a glorious melange. Dig or till to a depth of at least one foot, and keep mixing until the amendments are well incorporated. If mixing by hand, a short, square-tined garden fork may be just as efficient and far easier to handle than a shovel, which can get heavy very quickly.

PLASTIQUE RECYCLE
100%
PLASTIC

EIGHT

# MULCHES AND COMPOST

## Making Mulch and Compost— Feeding Plants and Combating Weeds

*Creating planting areas is just the first step in garden-making. Feeding and weeding these plants we install will be ongoing chores that greatly affect the health and good* looks of the garden. We can simplify those tasks by building our beds properly and by using both weed-suppressing and feeding mulches.

When and how to feed our plants is an absorbing question for gardeners. Dozens of commercial fertilizers exist, all making rival claims on our attention and our wallet. Some plants have very specific needs, but most are content with a fairly simple and straightforward nutritional regimen.

*Compost can be made on any scale, from vast windrows of recycled sewage sludge to tiny quantities of dried leaves and moss. This gardener stockpiles all sorts of ingredients for her hand-mixed composts, which may include anything from dried cherry stems to aged oak leaves, pine needles, charcoal, or even kitty litter (unused, of course). (Garden of Connie Caunt, Victoria, British Columbia.)*

*In mixed borders, where trees and shrubs are joined by perennials, bulbs, and ground covers, early feeding ensures a good spring and summer performance. If we wait too long, rising perennial foliage will prevent even application of feeding mulches. Late winter is also a terrific time to get the jump on weeds. (Garden of Margaret de Haas Van Dorsser, Portland, Oregon.)*

Spring and fall are the traditional times to feed plants. Spring feeds are fast-acting, offering rapidly growing plants the nitrogen they need for a solid summer performance. In fall, top growth slows down or halts altogether. This is the time to feed roots, which continue to stretch and grow underground despite low temperatures.

Homemade fertilizers have several advantages over commercial ones. They are relative cheap to make in bulk, and can be designed to promote slow, steady growth instead of dazzling but overly lush bulk that rarely ages well. Concentrated commercial fertilizers can badly burn or even kill young or winter-stressed plants, while mild homemade ones are safe even for convalescents. What's more, organically based homemade feeds condition and enrich the soil.

All plants, but especially young ones, develop best when given healthy soil and growing conditions. They

*By midsummer, many plants can use some replenishment. Overfeeding with nitrogen-rich commercial blends can stimulate an excess of leaf growth at the expense of flowers, but a balanced organic feeding mixture keeps flower production high. Mixtures of aged manure, compost, and alfalfa (whether pellets or in bulk) provide a slow but steady supply of nutrients. (Garden of Tom Chakas, Berkeley, California.)*

need ample elbow room to develop their proper shape and size. They need air and light. They need adequate and regular supplies of water and food. Though some chemical foods are marketed as time-release, few people realize that the release only begins to occur when soil temperatures reach between 70 and 80°F. Where springs are slow and cool, plants aren't getting any good from those little capsules until July.

A good feeding mulch will contain both soil amendments and some readily available nutrients. Where I garden, local soils tend to be high in potassium, but low in phosphorus. Both bone meal and rock phosphate will increase phosphorus levels, the former immediately, the latter over time, so they are generally used in combination. For soils that are low in nitrogen, we can add seed meals like cotton and soy. I often use a combination of aged manure and alfalfa pellets, both of which are fine tilth boosters as well.

*Pots and container plantings must be fed regularly all season long, since nutrients are flushed out quickly by repeated waterings. Even raised beds and oversize containers large enough to hold trees suffer from this situation. Give any such plantings a booster of feeding mulch in late winter or early spring to start them off right, then follow up with frequent liquid feedings as long as they remain in active growth. (Garden of Linda Beutler, Portland, Oregon.)*

In my garden, I modify the native soil's acidity with dolomite or agricultural lime. My mother, who gardens on alkaline hardpan, also adds plenty of neutralizing compost, but she uses gypsum (which can come from old wallboard) to encourage her heavy soil to develop a finer grain and to boost the naturally low levels of calcium and sulfur.

Anywhere you garden, your feeding mulches should contain compost, which is nearly always neutral in pH. A good range of trace elements and minerals are found in kelp meal, another common feeding mulch ingredient.

## TOP MULCH AND FEEDING MULCHES

So what's a top mulch? In established gardens, plants get tucked in for their winter rest with thick blankets of humus builders such as compost and aged manure. Top mulches are added in thinner blankets, only an inch or two at a time. Made of shredded bark or chopped leaves, aged sawdust, or even gritty gravel, these protective mulches also improve the soil, but their primary purpose is different.

Top mulches prevent or reduce runoff, keeping soil amendments like manure in place. They also suppress weeds (which never seem to stop growing), insulate tender plants from winter chills, and keep spring flowers from getting mud splashed.

Top mulches also conserve moisture. In a wet winter, it's hard to imagine that this is a genuine concern, but in autumn, when the top mulch is applied, it can be. After a dry summer, plants are often stressed by drought. If they go into winter too dry, they are more susceptible to winter damage than plants with adequate water reserves. When autumn rains are slow in arriving, we must water the beds and borders deeply before adding the top mulch.

The approach of spring means it's time to start mixing up another kind of mulch. As our

*Spring feeding mulches of aged manure and alfalfa can be applied anytime after the snow cover retreats. It's much easier to spread feeding mulches evenly when top growth is still small. Rising bulbs can be given an additional handful of bark or straw mulch to protect emerging buds from late frosts and guard early flowers from mud splash. (Garden of Margaret de Haas Van Dorsser, Portland, Oregon.)*

### SPRING FEEDING MULCH

The following recipe is measured by volume, using a tub or bucket to equal one "part." Mix it up in a wheelbarrow, then store the mix in a tightly closed garbage can.

*2 parts large, untreated alfalfa pellets*
*1 part aged manure (bagged is fine)*
*1 part compost*

Some nurseries and most hay and feed stores carry alfalfa pellets in fifty-pound bags, which cost around eight dollars. Get the big pellets used for feeding calves and goats, but skip the steroids—get the nonmedicated kind. One fifty-pound bag is enough (in combination as above) to feed about 200 square feet of border.

To spread the mixture, toss it about as if you were throwing a Frisbee (or feeding chickens). The idea is to distribute a fairly even layer over the entire planting area. Unlike commercial fertilizers, which can be so powerful that they actually burn young plants if used too generously, feeding mulches are mild enough to use in quantity. Don't get too carried away, though; no matter how hungry, no plant likes being smothered with lunch. Be sure the crowns of young or small plants can breathe freely.

plants begin to stir and stretch, they need a good breakfast to help them gather energy for their annual performance. Feeding mulches provide a steady supply of nutrients for garden plants, combining a quick fix of nitrogen with slower-acting soil builders. The simple mixture outlined above is good for almost any garden situation. You can scatter it generously through established borders, in shrub beds, and around mature trees, which will all benefit from the soil conditioners as well as the instant gratification.

The combination of alfalfa and manure is synergistic, so that a greater portion of their nitrogens become available to plant roots when they are used in tandem. Greedy feeders like roses and clematis love the immediate boost this mix gives them. Vegetable starts and soft fruits like strawberries are also appreciative recipients of this spring feed.

You can broadcast it in new beds, covering the surface with an inch or so of the mulch. In established beds, give each plant a handful or two, depending on size. Under trees, spread the mixture out to the drip line. You can also toss it evenly over a tired lawn for a refreshing wakeup call.

## Booster Feeds

While most feeding mulches can be added to any kind of garden freely, with little worry about overdoing things, organic booster feeds are a bit different. These are more concentrated nutrient sources that are placed above the root zones of each plant.

This careful placement avoids wasting fertilizers, which often end up polluting our waterways rather than feeding our plants. Used carelessly or to excess, chemical fertilizers are a significant source of nonindustrial pollution. Surprisingly, more comes from home gardeners than from farmers, who can't afford to waste expensive supplies.

One of my favorite booster feed recipes originated at the Territorial Seed Company. This wonderful mail-order company specializes in regionally appropriate vegetables for gardeners west of the Cascades, though they also have a national catalog of vegetables, herb, and flower seeds. Their founder, Steve Solomon, is an inspired and experimental gardener who is always pushing the gardening envelope. His all-purpose booster feed (right) can be used in ornamental borders or vegetable gardens. It's especially good for new gardens made where soil is depleted or unimproved.

### GENERAL PURPOSE BOOSTER FEED

This mixture, like the feeding mulch, is measured by volume. Use a lightweight scoop or bucket, blending the ingredients in the wheelbarrow. To keep the mixture fresh, store it in a watertight container (I use small, heavy-gauge plastic garbage cans).

*4 parts cottonseed or soy meal*
*1 part dolomite or agricultural lime*
*1 part rock phosphate*
*1/2 part kelp meal*

This blend is quite concentrated and contains both immediate and long-term nutrients. This is not a broadcast mulch; just scatter a small amount around each new plant and gently scratch it into the top inch or two of soil. A small plant, such as a transplant from a four-inch pot, would receive about a tablespoon of booster. A gallon-size plant would need a scant quarter of a cup, while a five-gallon shrub would get half a cup. A large, mature shrub or tree with an extensive drip line might need a whole cup or more. In any case, cover the scratched-up soil with a light top mulch of shredded bark or chopped straw to keep weeds down and maintain soil moisture.

## Mulching with Manure

My own favorite mulching material is pit-washed dairy manure. Indeed, few substances can rival the open texture and root-building qualities of this marvelous substance. Incorporated generously into clay or sand, it creates an excellent medium for plant growth. Used as topdressing, it makes a handsome mulch that keeps soils moist and cool come summer.

In dairy country, it's easy to find farms (or dairies) that deliver washed, partially composted manure by the truckload for a very reasonable price. Sometimes it's even free for the taking, if you have a truck to haul it in. Some people try to haul manure in cars and vans using tightly closed garbage cans. Let me tell you from experience, this is not a good idea. Even if you manage to get home without losing any cargo, the car will reek for months. If you do have a spill, you will discover that manure spills rival oil spills in their tenacity.

In my area, a ten-yard truckload of washed dairy manure runs about one hundred dollars, depending on the distance between you and the cows. In the city, delivery charges can run a bit higher, but the price is still usually competitive with that of other mulching materials.

## NEUTRAL SPRING BORDER BOOSTER

In many parts of the country, native soils are either acid or alkaline. There are thousands of plants that will adapt happily to either condition, but some universally popular vegetables and ornamentals grow best when such soils are buffered by neutral composts and mulches. The following border booster is designed to make both natives and exotics happy. Use it on vegetable plots, mixed borders, and established shrubberies containing native plants.

*5 parts compost*
*4 parts cottonseed or soy meal*
*1/3 part raw bone meal*
*1/3 part steamed bone meal*
*1/2 part kelp meal*

Two kinds of bone meal are used, because they act differently: Steamed bone meal is available to plants right away, while raw bone meal breaks down slowly. Spread this booster feed thinly around each plant, extending in a circle to the drip line of shrubs. Allow a small handful (about a quarter cup) per plant, adding more (one-half to one cup) for larger shrubs. Lightly scratch the booster into the top inch or two of soil, and cover it with a thin top mulch.

Composted cow manure is in many respects superior to the common run of soil builders and mulches. Unlike bark, it has no splinters. Unlike pine needles, it is not acid, but nearly neutral. Unlike sawdust, it carries its own supply of nitrogen in the form of urine, which is premixed with the manure at no extra charge (those kindly cows are always happy to please).

A light, fluffy substance that opens tight soils and helps keep sandy ones moist, composted dairy manure is the first amendment in all of my gardens. Indeed, it is sometimes the only one needed to get started in garden-making, since it can be used equally well as a soil amendment, topdressing, or mulch.

While most animal manures are beneficial (cat and dog ordure are obvious exceptions), they vary somewhat in quality. Dairy manure has several distinct advantages besides those already mentioned. For one thing, cows have many stomachs with which to digest their food. Thus their manure has few if any of the weed seeds that plague horse manure.

Washed and composted cow manure has an attractively uniform texture that feels pleasant to the hand and works wonders on tired soils. Goat or rabbit manure will too, but those little pellets take longer to break down. The squeamish may well find themselves shrinking from doing hand work among the bunny droppings. (As previously mentioned, it is wise to use gloves when handling manures of any kind, which can harbor unfriendly bacteria.)

*Established shrub beds don't need to be redug or disturbed in spring. A light topdressing of compost will act like a mulch, opening crusted soil, conserving moisture, and renewing the supply of nutrients. (Garden of Margaret de Haas Van Dorsser, Portland, Oregon.)*

*Meadow plantings of alpine and dwarf plants can be difficult to care for unless there are plenty of safe places for the gardener to step. Careless tossing of coarse feeding mulches can easily rot the sensitive crowns of many alpines, so nutrient mixtures must be spread by hand, taking care that no small emerging plant is accidentally covered up. (Garden of Ernie and Marietta O'Byrne, Eugene, Oregon.)*

As for pig and chicken manure, they are far too chemically hot to use directly on any kind of garden. Both need significant composting before they are ready for use, or they can burn plants rather than feed them. What's more, both smell exactly like their creators for a long, long time. If you have a ready supply of any of these manures, incorporate them into the compost pile before use. Over time, their obtrusive qualities are mellowed through the cooling-down period.

### *How Much Manure?*

How much you will need varies, depending on the size of your garden and the state of your soil. In general, one eight- to ten-yard load will suffice for a small new garden. A medium-size garden on a standard city lot might need two or three loads, and a suburban lot larger than one hundred by one hundred yards could easily require five or six loads. If you are making a really big rural garden, you might want to buy some cows of your own.

Even ten yards of manure sounds like a lot, looks like a lot, and feels like a lot when you are on the small end of the shovel. However, this is one amendment that is hard to overdo. The only danger is that excess manure can pollute water supplies. To avoid this, make your manure pile where rain won't wash it into the gutter, open streams, ponds, or any waterways. (See Chapter 7, pg. 118, for more information about containing manure and protecting the water supply.)

In garden terms, any good animal manure is a multipurpose substance. Added to poor soil, manure improves the tilth and texture. In clay soils, added manure improves air flow and promotes good drainage, both of which encourage healthy root growth. In sandy soils, manure acts like a sponge, retaining moisture that otherwise escapes too quickly. Used as a topdressing, a thick layer of manure can smother weeds and discourage unwanted seedlings.

In summer, manure mulch helps keep soils moist, and in winter, it acts like a blanket, insulating plants from hard frosts.

Though aged manure is lower in nitrogen than hot, fresh manure, the latter isn't as safe for plants, which can be burned by harsh, raw nitrogen. As with feeding mulches, the modest nutritional value of aged manure can be increased by adding alfalfa pellets, which creates a synergistic release of extra nitrogen from both ingredients.

## COMPOSTING: RECYCLING THE GARDEN

No matter where you garden, it is likely that your native soils can stand some improvement. Though not itself high in nitrogen, compost improves the nutritional value of soils of all kinds. Acid soils in particular can be nutrient rich, yet unless humus is added, the nutrients are not fully accessible to most plants. As it breaks down, compost not only releases its own stored nitrogen, but also helps (through the action of tiny soil microorganisms) to change those soil-locked minerals and nutrients into forms more readily available to plant roots.

Since this takes time, the result is a slow, steady supply of balanced plant food. Unlike chemical fertilizers, organic supplements like compost and manure don't offer plants the hormonal rush of steroids. Mild and moderate, they patiently give of their goodness for months and even years.

For as long as humans have been cultivating plants, the most productive agricultural systems have been those which recycled. Ancient horticultural practices from many cultures shared the modern concept of biosustainability: Everything that comes out of the garden goes back in, one way or another. Everything the garden needs can be supplied from its own abundance.

Homemade compost is especially valuable as an amendment because it is teeming with microbial life. A chunk of compost the size of a quarter contains six billion microbes that feed our plants by feeding the soil. When we recycle the garden into compost, nutrients that would be lost are returned.

The more varied the raw plant material, the richer the microbial mix in the finished compost. Since over 6,000 different microbial life forms exist, each favoring certain plants, we can encourage microbial diversity by growing the greatest possible variety of crops. When we mulch with complex, plant-based composts, we nurture our soil, which in turn feeds our plants better than chemical fertilizers can.

Used as mulch, compost not only conserves soil moisture, but it turns the top few inches of soil into an ideal mini-climate for healthy microbial life. Best of all, that compost blanket forms a humidity bubble that captures carbon dioxide, which plants breath in and convert to oxygen. For plants, having lots of available carbon dioxide is similar to the effects humans feel when they breathe pure oxygen; it invigorates them and makes them grow more strongly.

### Practical Composting

At its simplest, composting is a slow process which can take several years. To speed things up, gardeners have devised many systems for encouraging beneficial rot. All incorporate the same general principles. The first is to put your pile where it will be unobtrusive, yet easy to use.

Even a small pile requires ample room; the minimum size is about four square feet. For an average garden, the optimal size is about twice that, and the most efficient shape is cubic rather than free-form: Compost bins are both tidier looking and more chemically efficient. Twin bins will work far better than a single pile. A set of two four-by-four bins make it possible to be building a new, active pile in the second one while using mature compost from the first bin for the garden. If your space is big—anything over about a quarter acre of garden—a set of three connected bins will be even better. The bins can be as big as you like, but remember that large ones are harder to fill and mix, especially if you aren't a very large person.

Another major consideration is surface area. Compostible materials like grass clippings or fine-textured leaves can be added directly to the compost pile. Big leaves and large stalks and stems need to be reduced in size before they go on the heap. Smaller bits break down much faster than big ones; by creating more surface area, you can significantly assist the decomposition process.

The usual way to do this is with a leaf shredder, or by running over heaps of leaves with a lawn mover. The fun way is with a machete or brush-clearing knife. As you whack away at big piles of garden detritus, you can feel your tensions draining away. Either way, the result is a more uniform mixture of ingredients which can rot happily together.

What you mix into your compost heap is also important. The traditional rule is to use half green and half brown ingredients. That means for every wheelbarrow load of fresh grass clippings, you need to add an equivalent quantity of

*In this tiny garden, nothing is wasted. Every possible resource is harvested and reused, from leaves and grass clippings to the very stems and twigs of the old cherry tree overhead. This pathway is made from salvaged sticks and stalks that are dried and cut to size. (Garden of Connie Caunt, Victoria, British Columbia.)*

something like dried leaves or chopped straw. The idea is that the nitrogen in the green stuff is balanced by the carbon-based brown stuff.

While kitchen scraps can contribute a rich variety of microingredients, stick with the fruits and vegetables. Adding meat, fish, or even dairy leftovers to compost is a standing invitation to rats and raccoons, not to mention wandering dogs.

Garden weeds are welcome so long as they aren't heavy with seed (which can persist and cause you worse weed problems when you reapply them to the garden). Obvious exceptions are weeds that spread by root, shoot, and seed. Things like bindweed (*Convolvulus* species, also called wild morning glory), stinging nettles, brambles, and the running grasses are all dreadful pests in the compost or in the garden. Bag these and discard them into the trash, or add them to the burn pile.

A properly made compost heap will get hot enough to cook most weed seeds as well as nasties like fungal diseases and bacterial blights. For a quick start and a sustained slow burn, begin your first pile in layers. If you use bottomless bins set right on the earth, start by scratching up the soil surface a bit. This makes a better interface between the soil and the compost, allowing water, air, and beneficial soil microbes to pass freely back and forth.

The first layer is a brown one, comprised of materials that are already well on their way toward decomposition. Dried leaves, grasses, and garden leftovers can be spread out flatly on the stirred soil to a height of about six or eight inches. Next, spread on the same amount of greens. Repeat the process, making a lovely layer cake of garden grunge, topping it off with a carbon-based batch of browns for icing.

If your brown materials are dry, sprinkle each new layer with water. The idea is for the entire mass to be moist (but not dripping) to encourage rapid decay. Cover the pile with a burlap sack, a sheet of heavy plastic, or a piece of tarp to maintain that optimal moisture level.

Once your compost pile is made, its next requirement is air; like fire, the inner heat of compost cookery requires plenty of oxygen. Within a few days, you will discover that your new compost heap has started to cook. It will feel noticeably warm to the hand, and you can even see steam rising from it (during the cooler months, anyway).

An active compost pile can poke along on its own with no more help from you. However, unless more air is added, the process can take many months, especially in cold weather. To speed this up dramatically, just stir everything up a bit. Turning the compost heap ventilates the pile and reactivates the heat, just as pumping air into a fire with a bellows increases its temperature.

Strictly speaking, "turning compost" means exactly that: turning the pile over and redistributing the cooler outsides and the hot middle. In practice, it usually also means moving the pile from one bin to the next. When one bin is full, you simply transfer the pile to the empty side. If both bins are full, you just muddle things up as best you can. The idea is to get more air into the mix, so technique is not critical. It will be much easier to manipulate the matrix with a pitchfork or a lighter manure fork than with a shovel.

The only essential here is that the compost be recombined so that the dry, outer parts get thoroughly blended with the hot stuff from the center. If the compost seems dry, sprinkle on a little more water during the turning, and recover the pile when you're done.

The first turning is usually done when the pile's heat diminishes, which can take anywhere from a few days to a week or so after start-up. This first turn will reactivate the compost, which will heat up again quickly. Two or three weeks later, another heat decrease will signal the need for more air. Turn the pile again, bringing the outer portions into the center as before. Already you will notice a homogenization taking place; the stuff looks less like individual ingredients and more like compost.

If you repeat this process each time the pile cools off, you will make about four or five turns and have handsome compost within two or three months. If you don't turn it at all, you will have usable compost within six or eight months. The outer parts of an unturned heap will not be really "done," however, and can be stirred back into the next heap for further decomposition. There are often a few big chunks in the middle that need a little more time as well, so toss these back in the heap as they turn up.

Many people are highly disappointed when they make that last turn and discover that finished compost isn't as perfectly textured as potting soil. Indeed, some folks get quite upset and decide they must be doing something wrong. The truth is, real compost is lumpy.

To make that lovely, uniform stuff you see in the magazines, you need a soil sieve or screen. These are just what they sound like—tools for dividing the rough from the smooth. Soil sieves are smallish pans inset with heavy-gauge wire mesh, usually in half- or quarter-inch screen. These can be held in your lap while you sift compost into a pot, or placed over a bucket. To use a soil sieve, scoop in some compost and rub it through the holes. (This always reminds me of making applesauce.) The result is fine enough to use for starting seeds or transplanting tiny seedlings.

Soil screens are larger, flat versions of the same thing. Generally square or rectangular, they are designed to use over a wheelbarrow or cold frame. They are most often coarser than sieves, with one-inch or three-quarter inch mesh. Toss a few shovelfuls of compost on top, then run it through the screen with the back of the shovel (flat blades work best). This is working compost, ready to dig into bed or border, or use as a feeding mulch anywhere in the garden.

As soon as one bin gets emptied out, start a new pile. You can stockpile materials until you are ready to start the layering again, covering the piles with a tarp to keep them damp and neatly in place. The rhythm of compost-making echoes the rhythm of the gardening year, slowing down in winter, accelerating in spring, moving briskly in summer, then tapering off in fall. Like the garden itself, compost slumbers during the coldest months. Its rebirth—the gentle steam that lets us know our pile is awake—becomes as much a harbinger of spring as the first snowdrops and snow crocus, and every bit as welcome.

NINE

# BUILDING BETTER BEDS AND BATTLING WEEDS

## How to Create Optimal Planting Places within the Garden

*The best way to have a terrific garden is by making dirt into terrific soil. It's equally important to make that soil into practical and attractive places, beds, and borders where we can readily arrange our chosen plants.*

Sometimes this means remaking elderly beds that have lapsed into lawn. In a brand-new garden, it usually means creating entirely new garden beds. As previously discussed, bed-making is easiest when the ground is soft and moist with seasonal rains. When summer has baked the earth to adobe, it isn't much

*Where weeds persistently congregate—typically between pavers, in the cracks of brickwork, or along the edges of beds—take a note from nature. Remove the weeds, but replace them with a plant you like better. English terraces, patios, and paths are often tufted with small plants that relish the warmth and reflected light from paved surfaces. (Garden designed by Jeff Glander, Tacoma, Washington.)*

fun to break ground for a new garden. If you want to start your garden in the summer and can't wait for the autumn rains to soften that impenetrable dirt, set the sprinkler over the proposed area and let the water slowly soak in.

On very dry ground, water tends to run off rather than penetrate, so keep the water pressure very low. It can be useful to soak the area once by hand, allowing half an hour or so for the water to soften that top inch of dirt before setting the sprinkler in place. Perforated hoses, sometimes called leakers, will also saturate hard ground nicely. Where long-neglected soil or hardpan is deeply dried out, it can take a couple of days for this slow drip to soak in.

## STARTING WITH A CLEAN SLATE

Once the ground has been softened to a depth of at least six or eight inches, you can begin to work. If the new bed is covered with turf, cut it in long slices about twelve to eighteen inches wide. Pull up one short end and push forward, pulling as you go. Once the roots are broken, tight grass can be rolled up like a jelly roll. This is rather fun, and you can often get the kids to do it.

If you don't want to use the turf elsewhere, you can compost it in a sort of grassy sandwich. Lay the first strips green side down in an out-of-the-way corner. The next layer will run across them lengthwise with their green sides facing up. (Cut the strips in halves or thirds if they are too long.) Keep crisscrossing the strips in this fashion, matching grass to grass and dirt to dirt. Wet down the layers as you go, then cover the resulting mound with a layer of dirt. Top the whole with a tastefully colored tarp,

*Where an old lawn is cut up into small beds, it can be difficult to tend the remaining grass. To simplify care, make larger beds and reduce the grass to paths the width of your mower. Better yet, remove the grass entirely and replace it with a material such as shredded bark or gravel that requires no care. (Mackey garden, Portland, Oregon.)*

and wait for the neighbors to ask who you have murdered. Let it molder for a season or two and you will discover a treasure trove of rich, crumbly compost.

Sometimes, sadly, this great jelly-roll trick doesn't work so neatly. In a new, from-scratch garden where turf has been recently installed, you really can roll up those wide strips the builder laid down with very little effort. A bit of root slicing with a sharp eding tool or a flat-bladed shovel may be required, but the hardest part of the process is stooping over.

Longer-established turf is harder to pry loose, but in most situations lawn grass remains shallowly rooted. When cut in strips and rolled, the grass comes up in solid mats with just a couple of inches of roots attached. The strong-handed can usually wrestle established grass strips out alone, particularly from light or sandy soils.

If the grass is growing in heavy clay, the removal process is much easier with two people. One slowly pulls back the gradually enlarging flap of turf as the other slices the roots off. The slicers

*It's very easy to make new beds over a tired lawn. If the turf has been tamed, you can heap raised beds right on top of the old lawn grass, which will be smothered out quickly by the new soil. Where wilder meadows rule, it's best to get the grass and weeds out first. (Garden of Nani Wadoops and Ron Wagoner, Portland, Oregon.)*

can entertain themselves mightily by imagining an irksome foe to be the recipient of that sharply directed energy.

Elderly lawns with a lot of weeds in them can be quite difficult to roll. Unlike young turf, old lawns are no longer tightly knitted tapestries of grass. They pull up not in smooth rolls but in awkward patches and clumps. Old lawns are best treated like rough meadows, which must be mown as closely as you can manage before root removal begins. Once trimmed, the turf may then be dug over by hand or machine to remove grass roots. Soil prep is such splendid exercise, that if you don't own a tiller, borrowing or renting one will seem like a very attractive option after a few hours of root removal.

Should the area to be cleared consist of rough meadow instead of mown grass, the jelly-roll trick definitely won't work. Here, you will need to mow the grass as closely as possible, then dig out the roots. If the bed is bigger than a breadbox, you will probably prefer mechanical assistance; this is where a tiller comes in very handy. Don't be disappointed if you can't convince your turf to roll up and go away. The real goal is not to make green jelly rolls, but to clear the new garden of roots and weeds.

If you are noticing a lot of weeds, it's worth taking a few more weeks to solarize the soil. This means giving it a good baking by covering the bed with plastic. Though I've seen people use almost anything for this, from old shower curtains to paint drop cloths, I think that clear, heavy-mil plastic (like Visqueen™) works best.

First, get down to the dirt, stripping away the grass. Next, till or dig the bed, then soak it deeply. Spread the plastic wrap over the moist soil and pin it down, using horticultural cloth stakes (the kind that look like giant staples). Finish the job by heaping extra soil over the edge of the plastic to seal it up. This makes a tent that will heat up like a little oven. On a hot, sunny day, soil temperatures inside can reach egg-cooking heights, just like a city sidewalk. It's also hot enough to kill off quite a lot of soil pathogens, fungal and otherwise, which could give your future garden trouble. Many weed seeds and lots of leftover weed roots will also perish during the solarization process, which takes five or six weeks. While you wait, enjoy the sun, reveling in the thought that it's doing your future weeding for you.

### Ousting Obnoxious Weeds

After you remove the plastic, your bed should at last lay beautifully bare; however, certain weeds—notably the taprooted sort—refuse to be displaced so easily. If the soil is infiltrated by pernicious weeds like morning glory, stinging nettles, Japanese bamboo or knotweed (*Polygonum cuspidatum*), or blackberries, get ready for some real work. It is imperative to eradicate any or all of these stinkers, or your new garden is doomed from the start. Taprooted weeds like dock and dandelions also have to be taken out completely.

This is a big challenge, but a worthy one, since every scrap of root left behind will return to haunt your future garden. Indeed, with real nasties like bindweed, morning glory, and creeping buttercup, the thinnest hair of overlooked root will proliferate like bunnies, producing dear, wee, baby weeds everywhere you don't look.

### Out, Out Damned Weed

In general, I'm no advocate of machismo, but with weeds, as with wicked warriors, the best defense is a good offense. Many folks complain that it is boring to spend so much time preparing the soil when the nurseries are full of enticing plants clamoring to be planted. However, this lengthy preparatory work is definitely worthwhile. Anybody who has done hopeless battle with creeping buttercup, insidious morning glory, or thuggish Japanese knotweed knows (too late, of course) the value of the preemptive strike.

After you've started the war on weeds by solarizing the soil, the next move is often repeated tilling. This process can daunt even the

*Weeding is easiest in well-mulched soil. Deep mulches soften heavy clay soils so that even deep-rooted weeds come readily to the hand, especially after a ground-softening rain. (The Northwest Perennial Alliance Border at the Bellevue Botanic Garden, Bellevue, Washington.)*

toughest weeds like blackberries and nettles by constantly interrupting their growth cycle and eventually exhausting their roots. It does not work with every plant; try this with Jerusalem artichoke (*Helianthus tuberosus*) and you'll be wholesaling the stuff in a few years. Indeed, quite a few garden weeds adore frequent stirring up of the soul, sprouting faster than ever each time you till. Hmm. What to do?

Several thousand years ago, a Chinese scholar named Sun-tzu wrote a classic manual, *The Art of War*. In it, he observed that in order to defeat our opponents, we must first understand them. To manage—if not defeat—our weeds, we have to know their ways and needs. Like garden plants, weeds come in various persuasions. Some are perennials, returning relentlessly from their deep roots year after year after year despite our best efforts to eradicate them (Canada thistles leap to mind). Others are annuals with astonishing powers of regeneration. Allowed to set seed, a single chickweed can re-create itself hundreds, if not thousands of times each year. Clearly, different strategies are called for in each case.

With ardent self-sowers, mowing is a good temporary control, since it inhibits flowering. Often, mown plants can be tilled under successfully. A thick mulch will inhibit resprouting of many annual weeds, which often need light to germinate.

Taprooted troublemakers like dock and dandelions can be very hard to uproot fully. When cut close to the soil surface, the roots resprout faithfully. To avoid this, use a long, thin-bladed weeder, an old kitchen knife, or a Japanese farmer's knife (sometimes called a *hari-hari*), notched on one blade edge and smooth on the other. Armed with this impressive implement, you can pry almost anything loose from the tightest soil. Cut away four or five inches of the root—the rest will rot in peace.

Where large patches of ground are infested, weed flamers are highly satisfying to use and can be amazingly effective on persistent weeds. However, it's hard to use this tool selectively in the garden (and flamers can be dangerous during droughts, when wildfires easily burn out of control). To avoid plant and property damage, save the flame throwers for paths and patios only. Furthermore, if you have teenage sons, do not—repeat DO NOT—allow them to do this part of the pest control for you.

If you don't enjoy flame-zapping weeds yourself, you have recourse to another method which is just as effective and far more genteel. In ornamental gardens, and anywhere where finesse and control count, the preferred heat treatment consists of boiling water, applied with a spouted teapot directly to the offending plants.

*Covert Operations*

One of the best ways to purge a large space like an entire garden bed of wicked weeds is by planting it with a cover crop. Pick something that grows faster than your weeds and the baddies will be crowded out. In England, potatoes were commonly grown as a cleansing crop where those velvety lawns were to be made. Few weeds could compete with the sprawling mats of potato foliage above ground and their tangled roots below.

The hitch to this method was that it took several years. The potatoes were followed by several secondary cover crops like winter wheat and clover which improved the tilth and nutritional value of the soil. Only after multiple crop cycles were those lush lawns laid down. These days, vegetable gardeners often smother weeds with winter cover crops such as buckwheat or alfalfa. Sown in the fall, they sprout quickly and keep growing until the first frost. Then, or in the spring, the cover crops are tilled under before they go to seed. As they rot, they release stored nitrogen for your new plants.

Clumping (nonrunning) clovers also make good smother-cover crops, because their roots form little nodules that fix nitrogen in the soil. After the clover's top growth has been tilled under, that nitrogen remains available for the plants of your choice.

My favorite weed control is the "lazy" method. Simply heap a mixture of green grass clippings and shredded dry leaves or straw on top of the area you want to garden. A layer two feet thick is not too much. This makes a mini compost pile that will work away quietly while you think about what you want the bed to look like. Almost anything already growing there will be smothered by that heavy a blanket, and no new weeds will grow through it.

Tall or leggy weeds like nettles and blackberries need firmer treatment, though. Unless

*Beds and borders that are packed full of compatible plants offer fewer opportunities to wandering weeds. Where weeds consistently recur, replace them with ornamental plants that have similar cultural requirements. Garden plants with deep roots (such as bush hollyhocks or lavateras) will grow happily anywhere dandelions do. Fragrant annuals like sweet alyssum willingly fill gaps left by annual spurges. Blue fescues thrive where clumping weed grasses prosper. (Garden of Ernie and Marietta O'Byrne, Eugene, Oregon.)*

they are fully covered by the compost-mulch, it only encourages them. In both cases, the solution is to first cut back their prickly top growth (wear serious gloves when you do this) and to dig out as much root as possible, which isn't easy. A short-handled mattock chunks out roots nicely, but the work is slow and quite hard. If you can't hire help for this, consider having the area tilled by a small tractor. Otherwise cut and mulch as deeply as possible. Keep your eye on the area, and recut stems as they appear.

Most effective of all is a combination of smothering, cutting, and digging. Start by cutting back tall weeds, then layer on the mulch. After a few months, the soil will loosen, making it easier to dig out roots. Discard them in the burn pile or trash—never the compost—and renew that mulch, keeping it at least a foot deep. Any stragglers which make it through that will be easy to pull out, but don't just yank; use a shovel or sharp mattock and remove all visible roots. In time, you will win the battle. If none of the above fully satisfy your urge to kill, more than seventy benign but effective weed control techniques are described in *The Gardener's Weed Book*, by Barbara Pleasant (Storey Publishing, 1996, $12.95). On the other hand, some of you may decide that when you can't really beat 'em, you might as well enjoy 'em. Most regions boast good weed books these days. In my area, for instance, *Northwest Weeds*, by Ronald J. Taylor (Mountain Press Publishing Company, 1990, $11.95), offers colorful photographs of the good, the bad, and the ugly. Savvy gardeners may elect to encourage the beautiful and good weeds and why not? Call the results a natural garden and you might just win an award from the ecoconservancy for your efforts.

# Garden Design Ideas

# URBAN CONDO

## A Year-round Entry and Patio Garden in a Tiny Space

*Entryways set the tone for both house and garden. This is the first thing visitors see and a sight you will see thousands of times yourself. In a small, urban space, it's important to* use both plants and structural elements that hold up well in all seasons.

A front entry is semipublic, tying your house and garden to the neighborhood. It's best to develop it in a style that won't look jarring or out of place with the greater surroundings. This doesn't mean you need to settle for bland uniformity, but unless you want to attract a lot of gawkers, the jungle garden or the model castle belong in the backyard.

The same things that make for good paths and patios make for satisfying entryways. Ease of access is at the top of the list; depending on your family life,

*Where ground space is limited, large pots or containers can make miniature gardens that welcome guests and define the entry of your home. Simple but structural topiary shapes have the potency of line to read well against classic or contemporary architecture.*

make sure your scheme allows room for a person with arms full of groceries, a bicycle, or a stroller, as well as kids and pets, who don't always look before they leap.

If you add paving, avoid fussy designs that confuse the eye. Visual simplicity and clear, direct paths work best here. So, too, do tightly set paving materials which create smooth surfaces that are comfortable and safe underfoot in all kinds of weather and in the dark. Automatic lighting which responds to sound and movement is another feature to be considered, for both safety and security.

If hardscape seems overly dominant, it can be softened with containers full of handsome, structural plants. Charming topiaries work well in entryways, or you can use large, permanent containers and fill them with an ongoing cycle of plants that rotate through the seasons. Again, in the interest of security it is wise to use containers which can be firmly fastened in place, so they don't vanish in the night.

*To create more visual interest, cluster pots in several sizes, choosing complementary shapes and textures. Large, complex pots look best with one bold, architecturally shaped plant, while smaller, clean-lined containers can hold more intricate arrangements.*

*Key evergreen plants remain in place all year round while a steady stream of seasonal color pours through the surrounding pots. Spiky yucca, bronze cordyline, and sculptural evergreens such as Chamaecyparis pisifera 'Boulevard' have enough character to make excellent anchor plants.*

Where space permits, a tiny oasis within the front entry creates a delightful change of atmosphere. A small fountain or water pot with a bubbler adds musical sounds which mask traffic noise. An arch or arbor can be hung with evergreen vines and flowery climbers that provide a flow of scent and color all year long.

*A small, inexpensive bubbler enlivens a plain water pot with sound and movement. Larger pumps can create little waterfalls or circulate water between a wall-mounted fountainhead and a splash pool on the floor. In a city courtyard, a two- or three-foot fall of water can mask traffic noise with amazing efficiency.*

# SUBURBAN NEIGHBORHOOD

## A Sunny Space for Flowers, Vegetables, Kids, and Pets

*Open and sunny, the suburban backyard can usually use a little enclosure to create visual privacy for the family. Screening fences may need to remain low to meet local* building codes, but often plain fence can be capped with trellis panels for slightly better coverage without violating the rules.

In this setting, it is often easier to use plants as architectural elements. Why not create a miniature arch of interwoven laburnums between the garage and the back porch? If your budget only permits a few big purchases, choose a small tree—perhaps a weeping cherry—which offers ornamental lines all year long. Once established, it can be threaded with several clematis to create scented curtains of blossom from spring into fall.

*Suburban yards are often empty canvases, awaiting the gardener's painterly touch. Plan your garden from inside the house, identifying key views to screen or preserve. Next, create entryways and paths. Consider adding a trellis-screened deck for outdoor dining and relaxing.*

Vines can be used to drape and disguise homely fences as well, whether chain-link or plain wood. A combination of evergreen climbers and summer bloomers—perhaps roses and honeysuckle—will create a lovely tapestry in every season. Woven across a broad arbor, grapevines create summer shade, often a shortage in newer suburban developments. Place a simple table and chairs beneath it and enjoy dining al fresco beneath the resulting bower.

Where vegetable gardens, play yards, and ornamental beds overlap, architectural elements like arbors and trellises can do double duty, defining and screening areas while supporting plants. This is even true of a lowly bean trellis: When well-made, it becomes a permanent structure that remains attractive in every season. Cleverly positioned, it can screen off the compost heap or block the view from a neighbor's window into the garden.

*A single good-sized tree like this weeping cherry will immediately create a sense of maturity, making a young garden look settled in. Low interior hedges will keep playful kids and stray balls out of precious plantings. Easy-going perennials mingle with fast-flowering perennials, herbs, and attractive vegetables in these multipurpose beds.*

*Where covenants forbid fences, a simple but structural bean trellis can create unobtrusive visual privacy by screening out unwanted views of neighboring properties. Use temporary structures to discover where such screening will be more useful, replacing them in time with more solid arbors or trellises planted with evergreen vines.*

Segregating kids and dogs into their own parts of the yard will reduce the heartache that results when contrasting world views collide. Enclose the dog-run as attractively as if it were another little garden, framing the entryway with sentinel shrubs or flanking it with big pots of dramatic plants. The play yard will probably need to be where you can keep an eye on activities, but a few trellis panels, a section of fence, or a short hedge can keep small feet and large balls out of beds and borders.

Family areas where everybody gathers to barbecue or lounge in the sun can be kept simple, with bold but minimal planting. This further reduces the probability of problems and makes being in the garden fun for all concerned.

DESIGN THREE

# RURAL RETREAT

## WORKING WITH SHADE, COMBINING NATIVES AND ORNAMENTAL GARDEN PLANTS

*Gardens that flow from neighborhoods into woods, meadows, beaches, or other natural settings need to balance the design demands of both environments. Generally, the* front of the house connects visually with the neighboring homes, so the front garden needs to reflect their styles to some degree.

The structural strength of home and street are often challenged by the strong lines of surrounding mature trees and shrubs. In these gardens, natural architecture is everywhere. Instead of adding lots of hardscape, the key is to create plantings that move the eye convincingly up to the treetops and back down to the relative intimacy of the garden.

*In rural settings, the garden becomes a link between the neighborhood and surrounding habitat. In wooded settings, new construction often removes the transitional plantings that link the canopy trees down to the earth. Restoring those shrubby layers creates a visual ladder for the eye and reconnects the garden to its natural environment.*

Homes in this sort of setting may have large back gardens which merge more or less gracefully into woods or native plantings of some kind. These transitions are of special interest, since this point of overlap is where many designs break down.

This is best resolved by altering the flow and feeling of the design and plantings, moving from more formal, contrived areas near the house to naturalistic, free-form areas as one approaches the wild. Bright, colorful, nonnative plants thus belong in the former category, while more subtle ones, or those with wildling charm, can be used to weave sensitive transitions between natives and exotic plants.

It's also worth combing nurseries for lovely natives that don't happen to be present in your garden but could cohabitate happily with those in place. Besides these, we can also seek out relatives of favorite natives, choosing those that hail from similar climate zones.

Quite often, the more open side of the house, the one that relates to the human world, is

*One or more large trees will make a powerful visual connection between the garden and its setting. Ornamental trees will look most appropriate near the house, while fast growing natives will echo the natural plantings in the nearby woods. The same pattern holds true for shrubs and perennials as well; ornamental plantings near the house may be relatively formal and incorporate mainly exotic plants, while those nearer the woods become less formal and include a greater proportion of natives.*

*Transitional areas can be edited, retaining handsome stumps and attractive native plants, but amplifying them with their allies from all over the world. As the shrubby, intermediate layers fill in, lawn areas near the woods can be replaced with evergreen ground covers punctuated with compact shrubs, perennials, and bulbs.*

fairly sunny. It makes even more sense to use this area for splendid colorful beds and bountiful borders that appreciate a sunny site. Those who enjoy basking may want to create some kind of enclosure here, so they too can relax in the sun.

The shade of mature trees and shrubs becomes a significant design factor in such gardens. Side and back gardens may need more than simple soil amendment in such sites, where root competition is already fierce. Horticultural barrier cloth can be laid down where you want beds and borders; this allows a flow of water and air but keeps those questing roots at bay.

To make your beds, just heap on new soil and plant away. To avoid smothering mature trees and shrubs, slope the soil down to crown level, holding it in place with more barrier cloth and adding a mild-mannered ground cover to keep it firmly in place.

# Index

Page numbers in *italics* refer to captions.


Acid soil, 109–10, 124

Alkaline soil, 109–10, 124

Amendments, soil, 108, 110, 111–19, 123–24. *See also* Compost; Mulches

Arbors, 33–34, *34*, 152, *154*

Arborvitae, *39*

Arches, *11*, 26

Art. *See* Garden art

Bamboo, Japanese, 141

Bamboo fences, *73*

Barberry, 63

Barrier cloth, 159

Beds and borders
- laying out, 101–3
- mixed, *51*, 52, *108*, *122*
- multipurpose, *152*
- sod removal, 138–41
- weed control, 141–45, *144*

Bellevue Botanic Garden, *108*, *113*, *116*, *117*, *142*

Benches, 23, 25, *26*, *31*

*Berberis* ssp. (Dwarf barberry), 63

Berms, 9, 11

*Betula pendula* 'Fastigiata' (White birch), 77

Bindweed, 133

Birch, 77

Blackberries, 141, 144–45

Bleeding heart, 107

Bobcat loaders, 84

Bones (structure), *31*, 55–60

Books
- *The Art of War,* 142
- *The Gardener's Weed Book,* 145
- *Gardens Are for People,* 50
- *Northwest Weeds,* 145
- *The Year in Trees,* 90

Borders. *See* Beds and borders

Boston ivy, 4

Bridal wreath spirea, 60

Bubble diagrams, 18–19

Buttercup, creeping, 141

Canada thistle, 142

Chain-link fences, 72, 74

*Chamaecyparis*
- *C. lawsoniana* (Lawson cypress), *39*, 42, 67
- *C. pisifera* 'Boulevard', *149*

Chase garden, *96*

Cherry. *See Prunus*

Cherry laurel, 59

Chickweed, 142–43

Church, Thomas, 50

*Clematis,* 74, 151

Clover, 143–44

Compost and composting, *121*, 131–35, 138–39

Construction projects, 79–87

Containers. *See* Pots and containers

Contractors, hiring, 84, 85–86

*Convolvulus* spp. (Bindweed), 133

Cordyline, *149*

Cover crops, 143

Dandelion, 143, *144*

*Deschampsia flexuosa* (Hair grass), 44

Designers
- Borroff, Dan, *11, 101*
- Burton, Pamela, *ix, 21, 23, 67, 100*
- Gauder, Konrad, *22, 81, 86, 89*
- Glander, Jeff, *17, 31, 47, 68, 137*
- Hammer, Nancy, *53, 62, 76*
- Mahar, Dulcy, *64*
- Pruden, John, *49, 54, 82*
- Schultz, Michael, *11, 17, 44, 75, 85, 107*
- White, Fred, *73*

Design ideas
- entry and patio garden, 147–50
- rural retreat, 155–59
- suburban yard, 151–54

*Dicentra* spp. (Bleeding heart), 107

Dock, 143

Doors, *4*. *See also* Entryways

Earth moving, 82–86

Elevation. *See* Grade changes

Enclosure, *12, 35, 36, 47*
- to create interest, 22–23
- from fencing, 71–74
- and garden rooms, 47–77
- partial, 25, 74–77
- for privacy, 34–36
- from walls, 69–70

English ivy, 72, 74

Entryways, *21, 22, 23*
- design ideas, 147–50, *148, 149, 150*

*Escallonia rubra,* 40

Evergreens
- for containers, *149*
- for framing views, *4*, 76–77
- for hedges, 60, 68–69
- for screening, 57–58

False cypress. *See Chamaecyparis*

*Fatsia japonica,* 42

Feeding. *See* Fertilizers

Fences
- bamboo, *73*
- chain-link, 72, 74
- enclosure from, *71*, 71–74, *73*
- for privacy, 35–36, *36*
- for screening views, *37, 38*, 39–40

Ferns, 107

Fertilizers. *See also* Humus; Manure; Mulches
- booster, 126–27
- commercial, 122, 123
- fall, 122
- homemade, 122, 126, 127, 128
- organic, benefits of, *113*
- spring, 122, *122, 125*, 125–26

Fescue, blue, *144*

Flamers, 143

Framing the view, 40–41, 74–77, *75, 76*

Garden art, *44*, 44–45

Garden bones. *See* Structure

Garden rooms, 47–55, *49*
- hedges for, 59–65

Gardens
- Bellevue Botanic Garden, *108, 113, 116, 117, 142*
- Beutler, Linda, *124*
- Caunt, Connie, *121, 133*
- Chakas, Tom, *123*
- Chase garden, *96*
- Chatfield, Lord and Lady, *34*
- Dyelle, Judi, *42, 71, 102*
- England, Elizabeth, *3*
- Garthwaite, Bobbie, *25, 28*
- Hardiman, Lucy, *1, 38, 70, 90*
- Heims, Dan, *33*
- Hidcote, 49, 52
- Hopper, Robin, *42, 71, 102*
- Hume, Cyril, *26, 34*
- Johansson, Shelly, *50*
- Lair, Elizabeth, *57, 83*
- Lonesomeville, *12, 59*
- Mackey garden, *139*
- Madrona Garden, *107*
- Murray, Valerie, *58*
- O'Byrne, Ernie and Marietta, *35, 51, 95, 105, 130, 144*
- Portland Japanese Garden, *61, 73*
- Raiche, Roger, *4, 7, 37*
- Smith, Lindsay, *36*
- Sullivan, Joe, *25, 28*
- Van Dorsser, Margaret de Haas, *122, 125, 128*
- Wadoops, Nani, *99, 140*
- Wagoner, Ron, *99, 140*
- Whitehead, Elaine and Dave, *39, 40, 79, 93*

*Ginkgo biloba* var. *fastigiata,* 77

Grade changes
- mapping, 9–13
- and paths, 21
- reshaping the land, *11, 79, 82*, 82–86, *83*

Grasses, 44, 53

Ground covers, 44

Hardscape, 9, 86–87
*Hari-hari,* 143
*Hedera helix* (English ivy), 72, 74
Hedges
  interior, *58*, 59–65, *152*
  lateral spread of, 60–61, *61*
  little hedges, 63–65
  perimeter, 58–59, *59*
  plants for, 58–65, 67–69
  for privacy, 34–35
  for screening views, *38*, 39–40
  shearing, 60, 64, *67*, 67–68
  spacing, 65–67
  tapestry, 52, 62–63
*Helianthus tuberosus* (Jerusalem artichoke), 142
Herbs, *3*, *93*
Hidcote, 49, 52
Holly, *59*, 63
Hollyhocks, *144*
Honeysuckle, 63, 74
Humus, 112–19
Hyacinth bean, 74
*Ilex crenata* (Japanese holly), 63
Imagining the garden, 31–34
Ivy, 4, 72, 74
Japanese bamboo, 141
Japanese farmer's knife, 143
Japanese holly, 63
Jerusalem artichoke, 142
Johnston, Lawrence, 49, 52
Journal, garden. *See* Notebooks, garden
*Juniperus* (Juniper)
  *J. chinensis* 'Columnaris', 77
  *J. communis,* 64
  *J. communis* 'Stricta', 77
  *J. scopulorum* 'Cologreen', 77
  *J. scopulorum* 'Skyrocket', 40, 65
  *J. scopulorum* 'Wichita Blue', 58–59
  *J. virginiana* 'Manhattan Blue', 59
*Kalmia*
  *K. angustifolia* (Sheep laurel), 63
  *K. latifolia* (Mountain laurel), 60
Kelp meal, 124
Knotweed, 141
*Lablab purpureus* (Hyacinth bean), 74
Laburnum, 151
Landscape fabric. *See* Barrier cloth
Laurel, 60, 63
Laurustinus, 59
Lavatera, *144*
Leach, David, 58
Lead contamination of soil, 110
Leaves, composting, 132
*Ligustrum* (Privet), 63
Lonesomeville, *12*, *59*
*Lonicera* spp. (Honeysuckle), 74
  *L. nitida* (Boxleaf honeysuckle), 63
Mackey garden, *139*
Madrona Garden, *107*
Magnolia, *28*
Maiden grass, 53
Manure
  amounts to apply, 130–31
  mulching with, 127–31
  nitrogen in, 131
  preventing pollution from, 118–19
  sources of, 116, 117–18, 127–30
Mapping the garden, 2–29
  basic techniques, 4–9, *7*, *8*
  bubble diagrams, 18–19
  elevation, 9–13
  enlarging maps, 17–18, *20*
  existing plants, 13–15
  hardscape, 9
  paths, 19–23
  plastic overlay for maps, 7, *20*
  utilities, 27–28
Master Gardener programs, 14
Mattocks, 145
Microclimates, 106–7, *107*
Mirrors, 41–42
*Miscanthus* (Maiden grass), 53
  *M. sinensis* (Eulalia grass), 68
Mixed borders, *51*, 52, *108*, *122*
Moisture zones, 106–7
Morning glory, 141
Mountain ash, 77
Mountain laurel, 60
Mowing, for weed control, 143
Mulches, 121–31
  feeding, 125–31

manure, 127–31
protective (top), 124–25, *142*

*Myrica californica* (Pacific wax myrtle), 59

Mystery, sense of, 22, *25*

**N**ative plants, 13–14, 156, *156*

Nettles, 141, 144–45

Nitrogen
in compost, 133
deficiency, 119
sources of, 119, 123, 131, 143–44

Noise, screening, 40, 54

Notebooks, garden, 7–8, 31–32

**O**utdoor living, 49–50, *50*

**P**achysandra, 44

Pacific wax myrtle, 59

Painted walls, 41

Paper
shredded, as mulch, 118
as weed barrier, 97

*Parthenocissus tricuspidata* (Boston ivy), 4

Paths, 19–23, 93–103
access, 19–21, *21*, *22*
brick and stone, *99*, *100*, *101*
constructing, 86–87
garden, *1*, 22–23, *25*
grade changes and, *11*, 21
grass, 94, *139*
laying out, *89*, 99–101
mapping, 19–23
mulched, *95*, 95–101, *96*, *133*, *139*
weed barriers for, 96–97

Patio garden, 147–50

Pavers, *93*, *101*, *102*, *137*

Pergolas, *34*

pH, soil, 109–10, 124

*Pinus mugo* (Swiss mountain pine), 42

Plant inventory, 13–15

Plants, buying, 26–27, 37–38

Pleasant, Barbara, 145

*Polygonum cuspidatum* (Knotweed), 141

Poplar, 67

Portland Japanese Garden, *61*, *73*

Potatoes, as cover crop, 143

Pots and containers, *1*, *148*, 148–50, *149*, *150*
fertilizing, *124*

Power lines, mapping, 27

Privacy, 34–36

Privet, 63

*Prunus*
*P. laurocerasus* (Cherry laurel), 59
*P. sargentii* 'Columnaris' (Sargent cherry), 77
*P. serrulata* 'Amanogawa' (Japanese cherry), 77

**R**aised beds, 9, 11, *18*, 19, 108, *140*

Red cedar, 58–59

Reshaping the land, 82–86

*Rhododendron,* 58

Rocks, *17*, *22*

Rooms. *See* Garden rooms

Roses, 4

Rudbeckia, *76*

**S**carlet runner bean, 74

Screening. *See also* Hedges
noise, 40, 54
plants for, 55–59
views, 36–41

Screens, soil, 135

Sculpture, *44* , 44–45

Seating. *See* Benches

Septic tanks, mapping, 27

Shady areas, *33*, 33–34, 42, 53, 159

Sheep laurel, 63

Shrubs, *17*. *See also* Hedges
borrowed, *25*
fertilizing, *128*
for framing views, 75–77
for structure, *31*, 55–58, *90*

Small spaces, *18*, *25*, *40*, 45, *90*, 147–50

Sod, removing, 138–41

Softstep™, 110

Soil, 105–19
drainage, 106–7, 108, *108*
improving, *108*, 109, 111–19, 131
lead contamination of, 110
pH, 109–10, 124
solarizing, 141
testing, 108–11
types of, 6, 105–7

Solarizing soil, 141

Solomon, Steve, 127

*Sorbus aucuparia* 'Fastigiata', 77

Spaces. *See* Garden rooms
*Spirea × vanhouttei* (Bridal wreath spirea), 60
Spurge, annual, *144*
Steps, 20, 21, *22, 82, 83*
Stinging nettles, 141, 144–45
*Stipa tenuissima* (Hair grass), 44
Structure (Garden bones), *31*, 55–60
Sunny areas, *3*, 6, *18*, 33–34, *34*, 52, 151–54
Sun-tzu, 142
Sweet alyssum, *144*
Sweet pea, 74
Swiss mountain pine, 42
Tape measures, 5
Tapestry hedges, 52, 62–63
Taylor, Ronald J., 145
Telephone lines, mapping, 27–28
Terracing slopes, *11, 79, 82*
Territorial Seed Company, 127
Thistle, Canada, 142
*Thuja occidentalis, 39, 67*
Tires, recycled, 110
Tools, for weed control, 143
Topiaries, 148–48
Traffic patterns, 6, *7*, 19–20
Transitional areas, *156*, 156–59, *158*
Trees
  choosing and planting large trees, 29, 87–91, *89, 156*
  evaluating existing, 13
  for framing views, *12, 25*, 75–77
  placement of, *27*, 27–29
  for structure, *31*, 55–58
Trellises, *57*, 152, *154*
*Trompe l'oeil*, 41
Utilities, locating and mapping, 27–28
*Viburnum tinus* (Laurustinus), 59
Views
  from benches, 25
  borrowed, *12*, 13, *25*
  creating, *40*, 41–45
  framing, 40–41
  from and within the garden, 38–39
  screening, 36–41
  from windows, 37
Vines, 74, 152. *See also specific plants*
Wallboard, recycling, 118, 124
Walls, 69–70, *70, 79*
  covering, *57*
  painted, 41
Water features, *17, 31*, 42, *42*, 53, *54*, 150, *150*
Weeds, 141–45
  barriers for paths, 96–97
  close planting for control of, *144*
  flamers, 143
  mowing, 143
  mulching, *142*
  between pavers, *137*
  seeds in compost, 133
  smother-cover crops, 143–44
  tilling, 141–42
  tools for removing, 143, 145
Weeping cherry, 151, *152*
Wind, 6
Windows, 3–4, *4*, 37
Winter gardens, *31*
Wood fiber, recycled, 110–11
Yucca, *149*

# ICE SKATING BASICS

by

**Norman MacLean**

Illustrations by
**Bill Gow**

With Photographs

Created and Produced by
**Arvid Knudsen**

**Prentice-Hall, Inc.**
Englewood Cliffs, New Jersey

Other **Sports Basics Books** in Series

**BASKETBALL BASICS** *by Greggory Morris*
**RUNNING BASICS** *by Carol Lea Benjamin*
**DISCO BASICS** *by Maxine Polley*
**GYMNASTICS BASICS** *by John and Mary Jean Traetta*
**RACQUETBALL BASICS** *by Tony Boccaccio*
**FRISBEE DISC BASICS** *by Dan Roddick*
**SWIMMING BASICS** *by Rob Orr and Jane B. Tyler*
**HORSEBACK RIDING BASICS** *by Dianne Reimer*
**SKIING BASICS** *by Al Morrozzi*
**BASEBALL BASICS** *by Jack Lang*
**FISHING BASICS** *by John Randolph*
**FOOTBALL BASICS** *by Larry Fox*
**SOCCER BASICS** *by Alex Yannis*
**SAILING BASICS** *by Lorna Slocombe*
**BICYCLING BASICS** *by Tim and Glenda Wilhelm*
**BACKPACKING BASICS** *by John Randolph*
**TENNIS BASICS** *by Robert J. LaMarche*
**TRACK & FIELD BASICS** *by Fred McMane*
**HOCKEY BASICS** *by Norman MacLean*
**BOWLING BASICS** *by Chuck Pezzano*
**KARATE BASICS** *by Thomas J. Nardi*



Book design by Arvid Knudsen

Printed in the United States of America · J

Prentice-Hall International, Inc., London
Prentice-Hall of Australia, Pty. Ltd., Sydney
Prentice-Hall of Canada, Inc., Toronto
Prentice-Hall of India Private Ltd., New Delhi
Prentice-Hall of Japan, Inc., Tokyo
Prentice-Hall of Southeast Asia Pte. Ltd., Singapore
Whitehall Books Limited, Wellington, New Zealand
Editora Prentice-Hall do Brasil Ltda., Rio de Janeiro

10 9 8 7 6 5 4 3 2 1

**Library of Congress Cataloging in Publication Data**

MacLean, Norman
Ice skating basics.

Summary: An introduction to the basic techniques of ice skating with information on equipment, exercises, and training for competitions.
1. Skating—Juvenile literature. [1. Ice skating] I. Gow, Bill, ill. II. Title.
GV849.M26 1984 796.91 84-6933
ISBN 0-13-448762-1

# CONTENTS


1. **All the World Enjoys Ice Skating** ........ **4**
2. **Getting Started: The Younger the Better!** . **7**
   How to Buy Your Ice Skates **8**
   Take Care of Your Skates **10**
3. **The First Basic Steps of Ice Skating** ..... **11**
4. **Techniques of Forward Skating** .......... **14**
5. **Techniques of Backward Skating** ........ **19**
6. **Recreational Skating** ................. **24**
7. **Hockey Skating** ...................... **26**
   Power Skating **28**
   How To Join a Hockey Team **29**
8. **Figure Skating** ...................... **31**
   Compulsory Figures **31**
   Ice Dancing **38**
   Free Skating **39**
9. **Speed Skating** ...................... **45**
10. **Your Future in Ice Skating** ............ **46**

***Index*** ............................... **48**

# 1 ALL THE WORLD ENJOYS ICE SKATING

The world of whiz and whirl is global—ice skating is the fun way to physical fitness around the world. From the earliest of times people everywhere have enjoyed and perfected the thrill of sliding across frozen water with some sort of runners attached to their feet.

Saint Lidwina is considered to be skating's patron saint. At the tender age of fifteen she broke at least one rib while skating on the frozen canals of the Netherlands and was invalided after that—performing several miracles from her bedside.



The great British ice star, John Curry with dancing partner, Catherine Foulkes in "La Valse."

The Edinburgh Skating Club in Scotland was founded in 1650, and was the first of its kind in the world. The first skating club in North America, the Philadelphia Skating Club and Humane Society, was formed in 1848.

Jackson Haines, an American ballet master by profession, revolutionized skating. He designed his own skates and translated his art onto the ice, learning how to do spirals on ice from ballet's arabesques, spread eagles from ballet's second position, and developing the sit spin.

Haines won the first two national championships in 1863 and 1864, but didn't receive as much acclaim as he thought warranted. He was to find true fame in Vienna. Skating to the music of Johann Straus, Haines made up up waltzes, marches, mazurkas and quadrilles, adding the grace and speed of skating to ballroom dancing—and also founding the disciplines of structured ice dancing and pair skating.

Vienna organized the first international skating meet in 1882, with twenty-three prescribed school figures, a special figure chosen by the skater and a four-minute, free-dance routine.

In 1876 the British managed to perfect the world's first successful artificial ice rink, the Glacarium in Chelsea. It worked by pumping a mixture of ether, glycerine, and brine through copper piping—and soon spread to other countries with rinks being ultimately built in New York, Vancouver, British Columbia, and throughout Europe.

The 1920 Summer Olympic games included ice skating, and were held in Antwerp. By 1920 Sonja Henie, a Norwegian, then eleven, made her Olympic debut, finishing eighth. At the time, skating and figure skating were the province of a small, rich aristocracy. Finally in 1928, Henie took the title away from Heima von Szabo-Planck—and for the next ten years was unbeaten—as her style and grace revolutionized skating everywhere.

The War brought a pause in the popularity of skating, but when it was over Dick Button dominated the field winning Olympic gold medals in 1948 and 1952—being the first to accomplish a triple-rotation jump.

In 1953 Tenley Albright became the first American woman to win a world title—and followed that up with the 1956 Olympic gold medal. Another American succeeded her, Carol Heiss, who married Hayes Alan Jenkins, World Champion, who was unbeatable from 1953 through 1956, when he won the gold. David, his younger brother who was equally skilled, won the Olympic gold medal in 1960.

While all this was going on, the Soviets were taking films and watching quietly from rink side. Ludmila Beloussova and Oleg Protopopov captured the Olympic gold medal for figure skating pairs in 1964 and 1968, but were surpassed by Irina Rodnina and Alexei Ulanov in 1972. Rodnina later changed partners to Aleksandr Zaitzev, winning ten world titles and three Olympic golds for figure-skating pairs, matching Henie's record of three Olympic gold medals in singles figure skating.

A tragic plane crash in 1961, in Brussels, Belgium wiped out the entire United States figure-skating team, but did lead to the hiring of the famous Italian, Carlo Fassi, to take over for three coaches who had died.

His first famous pupil was American superstar Peggy Fleming. Fleming won the 1968 Gold, despite a lackluster performance and the substitution of a single axel for a double and an unfinished double lutz. Janet Lynn, a pixie blonde, won five U.S. titles, but never a world title, but she has been influential in the sport nonetheless.

John Curry, the great British ice star, came along after that and dominated the Olympic games in 1976, winning the Olympic gold medal for figure skating.

Robin Cousins, also of England, succeeded Curry at Lake Placid in 1980, with Scott Hamilton winning the gold medal at Sarajevo, Yugoslavia, in 1984. Hamilton, a small, athletic American, trained at the Broadmoor, in Colorado Springs, Colorado, the unofficial capital of figure skating.

The best pair of skaters in the world, probably the best ever, are Great Britain's Jane Torvill and her partner Christopher Dean, who easily captured the Olympic gold medal at Sarajevo, in 1982 and 1983. The International Skating Union awarded them an unprecedented string of perfect marks, 6.0s, and they repeated this at Sarajevo to enhance their claim as the best ever.

But figure skating is only the tip of the iceberg. The Ice Skating Institute of America (ISIA) will tell one and all that only about one-half of one percent of skaters become good enough to pass even the most rudimentary of required figures. Yet almost everyone can learn to skate for fun and pass most of the easier ISIA tests which are part of the program at almost all rinks.

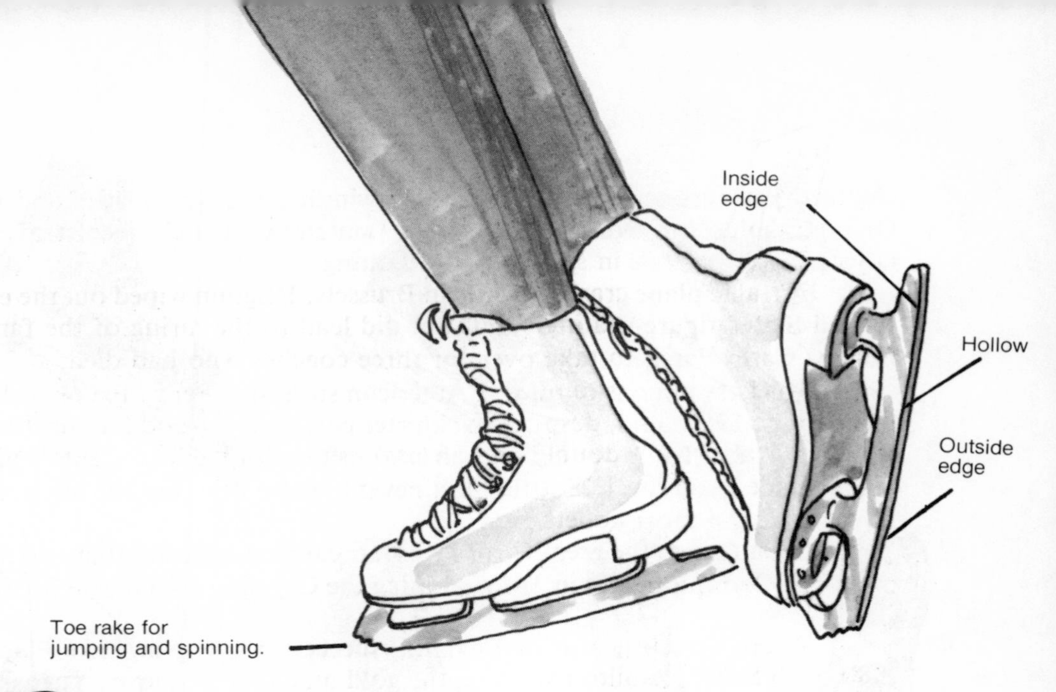


# 2 GETTING STARTED— THE YOUNGER THE BETTER!

To begin with, the younger you are when you learn to ice skate the better. The more natural you feel with your skates on the ice the more enjoyment potential there is and the greater the opportunities to advance in any specialty you choose.

Children at the age of two should be encouraged to skate. They can begin on double runners and graduate to regular single-runner ice skates within a year. If you haven't been on ice skates before, you are asking, "Can I learn by myself or do I need someone to teach me?" The answer is dependent on your desire to learn. No matter what the age, almost anyone can learn to skate.

In the beginning you should always have someone with you like your Mom or Dad, or an older sister or brother, or a pal. This is done for encouragement, sometimes for holding, and for demonstrating some of the basic methods of standing, walking, balancing, falling, and getting up. With a relaxed but determined attitude you will quickly master these elementary procedures.

Most of the local ice-skating rinks have classes for group instruction or private instruction available by professional teachers. Good skating depends upon good skates. Let's see what is needed.

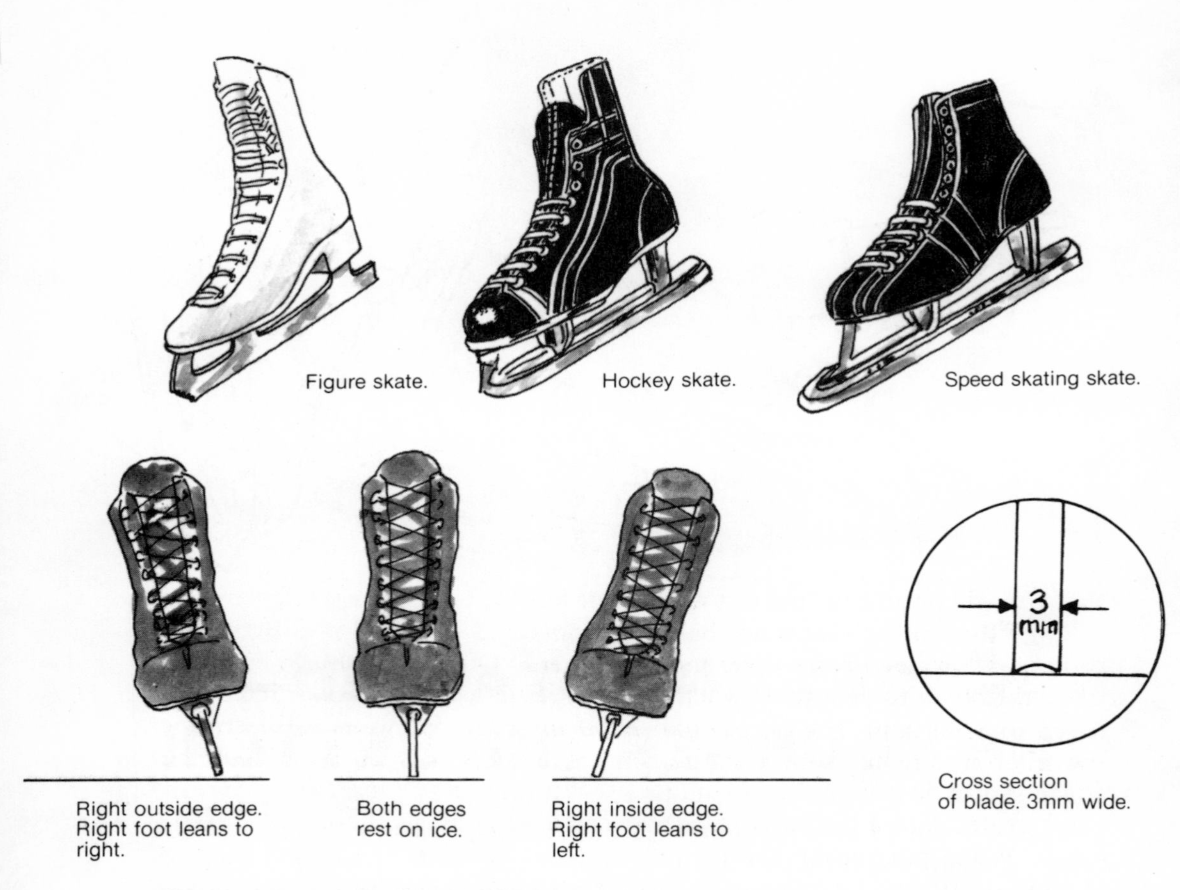


Figure skate.

Hockey skate.

Speed skating skate.

Right outside edge. Right foot leans to right.

Both edges rest on ice.

Right inside edge. Right foot leans to left.

Cross section of blade. 3mm wide.

## How to Buy Your Ice Skates

All skates, in order to give maximum support, must fit the foot snugly. The toes should just reach the tip of the boot, but not be cramped or curled under. Walking and/or skating should cause no up-and-down motion of the heel. A heel that is free to move will cause the skater much discomfort by permitting the ankle to bend freely, placing stress on muscles and tendons.

A quick check of the fit may be determined by looking at the laced boot. If the laces form a "V" from the toe to the lower calf, everything is in order. The large spread in the laces compensates for the stretch in the leather.

If you take the time to examine a pair of skates, you will find a gap between the eyelets. This gap allows for the stretching effect and assures the skater of snug boots.

Tight-fitting support is the greatest aid to any beginning skater. This comes from the boot having a good solid counter or support made of moisture-proofed leather or moisture-resistant fiber. Try running a finger along the rear of the boot from the heel to the instep. If the finger exerts enough pres-

Tightening the lace.

Testing the lace.

sure you will be able to find out whether or not the boot has a sturdy counter.

"Remember skates are basically boots and blades," says Peter Carruthers, a Sarajevo pairs silver medal winner. "Quality skates do cost. It is up to the buyer to determine whether a $35 pair is the right buy, a $60 pair or a $75 to $100 pair. The occasional skater might make do with the cheaper model or even rented skates, but remember the fit is everything and rented or cheap skates do not give an adequate fit. Without an adequate fit, you really can't skate. And a beginner, especially needs a good tight fit."

When purchasing skates, professionals consider the blades. A good skating outfit will have high-tempered steel blades. A good blade holds an edge over a longer period of time, presenting great savings in sharpener costs to the skater. Most likely, a factory-mounted blade will do with a beginner. You may buy your skates at the local pro shop or in a sporting-goods store. Both have some good points. For the occasional skater, the mass-produced skate may be more economical and serve the purpose. However, most pro shops do carry mass-produced skates as well as the more expensive brands.

**Clothing:** Your skating clothing is another factor in safety first, not only at the begining of your skating career, but all through it. Gloves can be worn at all times, not for warmth, but for safety. If you fall, they serve as a protection against the ice and against the possibility of being cut by other skaters' blades. Long pants, leotards, skating skirts, and tights are best for girls. Those parts of the body which may come in contact with the ice, in case of a fall, should be covered to prevent ice burns and scrapes. Regular pants, sweaters, or jackets are okay for boys. Tots should have waterproof padded snowsuits.

## Take Care of Your Skates

Everyone should have a protective scabbard or skate guard. This keeps the blades from getting nicked and dulled. Scabbards do not prevent rust. You must wipe your blades thoroughly dry after using them, or the rust will surely follow. Then put on the scabbards. When you get home, take the scabbards off to aid in the drying.

When walking on anything other than wood, rubber, or ice, always wear your scabbards. Concrete has ruined more skates than shoes.

Perspiration is the greatest enemy of the leather boot. If the boot is neglected, just like a shoe that is never polished and cleaned, it will become brittle and crack. A good leather preservative such as Lexol or a fine saddle soap, applied once a week to the inside of the boot, will keep the boot soft and supple. Any top grade polish will provide protection for the outside of the boot. In order to prevent rotting between the heel and sole, coat with a heel and sole enamel so that water cannot do its thing—rot the whole business.

Standing on ice. Walking on ice.

# 3 THE FIRST BASIC STEPS OF ICE SKATING

It is very important for the beginner to have plenty of time on the ice and to develop patience. Many potentially good recreational skaters give skating only *one try* and then chuck the whole thing. Failure to understand the basics of skating leads to disappointment or disaster. The key is to know what to do and what not to do.

**Standing:** To maintain your balance after stepping out onto the ice for the first time, you must keep your body's center of weight directly over your feet. Keeping your knees slightly bent or flexed and your hands waist high will help you keep your balance. Relaxing permits the center of gravity to shift continuously from one leg to the other as you begin to take your first hesitant steps.

**Walking:** Take small steps at first. The idea is to become accustomed to the ice and to accept or get used to that slippery surface under your feet and skates. Most beginners stay close to the rail or sideboard using the dasher for support. This is a safety factor, especially if there are other more skilled skaters using the rink at the same time. On a pond, of course, the assistance of an older person, Mom, Dad, or a pal, is helpful. Do not go out on the ice in the beginning without someone's watchful eyes on you.

Sculling. Two foot glide. Dipping. One foot gliding.

**Skating Forward or Sculling:** With your knees bent and both feet on the ice about six inches apart, point your toes outward and bring your heels together. This will place your weight on the inside edges of your skate blade. Now by applying the same amount of pressure to the inside edge of each skate, your knees will straighten slightly. When the blades are about as far apart as the width of your shoulders, turn your toes in and both feet back to a parallel position about six inches apart.

Then, increase the bend in your knee and flatten the blades on the ice. Point your toes out again and do the entire action over. The power or forward motion comes from the bending of your knees. Try and spread your feet as wide as possible.

**Gliding:** As your comfort increases on the ice and you begin to feel some assurance, you are ready for the gliding exercise. You can attempt the two-foot glide. Take three good steps and then let yourself glide on your two feet a distance equal to your height. Simply repeat this simple exercise until you are satisfied you have mastered it.

**Dipping:** This is a useful exercise for control on the ice. While you feel yourself gliding on your two feet, spread your arms to your sides and bend your body into the dip (or stoop) position. Keep your weight balanced. Don't stop—but raise yourself upright and glide a short distance. Repeat the dip a number of times until you can dip a little further down—and increase your speed. Keep your ankles straight at all times.

**Forward Swizzle:** Another good exercise to try is known as the forward swizzle. You glide a distance equal to your height in three in-and-out movements. Starting from a standing position you keep your toes pointed forward, then turn them to the side with heels touching. Bend your knees and stretch out your hands in front. Then bend a bit forwards from your hips and make your feet glide apart. Bring your feet together again by turning your toes toward each other. When bending your knees forward, push them forward.

The swizzle.

**One-Foot Glide:** You can glide now on two feet. So next try gliding with your right foot on the ice, then the left foot. It may feel awkward the first time you lift one of your skates from the ice and really are skating on just one blade, but this is what skating is all about. Speed doesn't come from walking or running on your skates. It comes from the pressure you put on the ice as you alternately lift and push off with your right and left skates. This is really the beginning of stroking on the ice. More on this a little later.

**How to Fall:** Staying on your feet, perfecting your maneuvers, and developing poise and balance on the ice is the object of skating but falls are part of the sport. So know how to fall and how to get up.

The best way to fall is from the dip position, letting yourself fall to the side and sliding on your rear until you come to a stop. Never fall on your hands. To get up, put both your hands steadily on the ice and by holding your left foot forward, bend the right knee until you feel yourself propped up by two hands and a knee. Slowly rise to a standing position and center yourself.

With patience and practice we have now accomplished the first basic steps of ice skating. From here on in we are ready to skate.

How to fall.

How to get up.

Complete turn to left.
One foot turn from start

# 4 TECHNIQUES OF FORWARD SKATING

It cannot be stressed too often that proper balance is the most important element of skating. As a beginner you must be conscious that the proper balance point over your blades for skating forward is just back of the center of your blades. You must hold your body weight in a direct line from head to toe. This means your head is up, your back is straight, shoulders relaxed, hips tucked under your body, and arms extended at about waist height.

**Stroking:** Now you are ready to learn how to glide over the ice with a series of moves alternating from one foot to the other. The actual forward motion comes from the part of the blade that is leaving the ice—and is therefore a push off.

With your feet in the so-called T-position (the heel of the right foot at a right angle to the instep of the left foot), anchor the inside edge of the left blade to the ice.

Bend your knees a bit extra and balance your weight over the arch of your left foot. Straighten your left knee, while keeping the right knee bent and switch the weight from the left to the right foot. Your left blade will turn and move you away from the whole side of the blade—and you will glide forward on your right foot.

You should glide forward with your shoulders and hips held square to the blade on the ice. After a short glide you will start to slow down or maybe even lose your balance. Bring your feet together. When your feet come together, turn the right skate out to about 45 degrees, catching the inside edge on the ice, and transfer the weight to your left foot as you push off with the whole side of your right blade.

In the beginning don't try to push with the blade that is leaving the ice. Try to keep your arms level, your knees bent, and your body straight. Do not use the toe pick to push off.

Keep your back straight and try to lengthen your strokes, with better timing of the knee bend and push.

**Forward Crossovers:** When you reach the stage in your learning process that you are ready to attempt to cross over and not just glide around a turn, you have truly made progress. You *must* learn to cross over properly if you really are to claim that you can skate.

Crossovers are a series of open strokes, followed by cross strokes, open, cross, open, cross, open, cross, etc. They are used to turn or round corners, or to skate in a circle. They also aid in building speed when you have become a more proficient skater.

Since most rinks skate in a counterclockwise direction, most skaters learn to do crossovers this way, but can't do them clockwise. You must practice in both directions as often as possible.

It is easier to practice crossovers in a circle when you first start. Try your first open stroke to the left, gaining a left forward outside edge, with

Doing a forward crossover.

right arm and shoulder forward and your right hip pressed down. Your skating knee (the left) should be deeply bent at the time of each stroke, with your lean remaining towards the center of the circle. Try and maintain these positions throughout your crossing over, so that you skate smoothly.

During each stroke your weight will be on an outside edge. The cross stroke consists of passing your right or free foot around and *in front of the toe of your left foot*, placing it on an inside edge and transferring your weight. When the right foot assumes the weight, bend your right knee as deeply as you bent your left knee on the open stroke, straighten your left knee and push off with the left outside edge. This thrust should be made outside the curve. As you push off, try holding this position to get comfortable doing it—and try to maintain it. The power you will get in this series of strokes comes from this push from the outside edge.

To continue, bring the free left foot from its extended position back to a parallel position opposite your skating foot. Keep it straight by straightening your skating foot. Now bend your knees and stroke off onto the left forward outside edge, getting thrust from the inside edge of the right skate as it lifts off the ice.

**Edges:** By now you understand what the inside edge of your blade is —and also the outside. Four basic edges can be skated with each foot—forward outside, forward inside, backward outside, and backward inside.

**The Forward Outside Edge:** Learning how to skate on your forward outside edges is a bit more difficult than skating on your forward inside edges which you have already learned how to use in stopping. If you start by gliding on both feet in a curve to the right around an imaginary circle, feet close together and body leaning to the right, as a steering guide, you will get the idea.

Glide with more and more speed in this curve a few times. Then, with your right hip, shoulder, and arm leading and your left shoulder back, bend your knees, and while keeping your body straight, lean towards the center of the circle you have created.

The blade closest to the center (the right) will be on its outside edge and the left blade will be on its inside edge. Raise your left foot now and hold it over the tracing you have made in the ice behind you, with the heel just inside the curve. Your left hip *must* be held back and kept down, tucked in behind the left shoulder. Try to make sure your body lean forms a straight line from the top of your head to the edge of your skating blade. When your forward outside edge feels reasonably secure on the right foot, do the entire process on the left. Learning on both left and right will take considerable time and practice.

**Alternating Right Forward and Left Forward Outside Edges:** If you think of these as swing rolls they are easy to learn. They can be a great plus that a figure skater brings to hockey, and play an important part in figure dance moves of an advanced nature.

As you skate forward on your right outside edge, always keep your hips and entire body in a neutral position facing your line of travel. Beginners sometimes tend to hold the free foot somewhat to the side. It should always be directly behind your skating foot, or directly in front of your skating foot. In a swing roll your free leg moves forward and is extended and held for a moment in front of your skating boot; then it is brought back alongside the skating boot.

Then, transfer your weight to your left foot, bend your knees and lean your body to the left. Turn your right foot onto an inside edge. Then, stroke out onto your left outside edge.

As soon as you can manage it, you should do these consecutive edges along a long axis, an imaginary line in which you trace (skate) half circles of about the same size alternating from side to side.

**Alternating Right Forward and Left Forward Inside Edges:** As a beginning skater you will probably find inside edges easier than outside.

Begin with both feet on the ice gliding to the left. Your body should lean towards the center of an imaginary circle, with the skate nearest the center of an outside edge, and the skating farthest from the center on an inside edge.

Now your shoulders and hips must be square to your line of travel. Your left arm is allowed to move slightly forward outside the circle, while the right arm remains outside of the curve. Palms are always held down. Your knees are bent and only your head is facing towards the center of the circle. Now, switch your weight to your right foot entirely, and move your left leg back so that your free foot is held inside the tracing. The heel of your left foot should be directly over the tracing.

If you rotate your arms, shoulders, and head to the left and bring your left foot forward, it should pass your skating foot closely, if not actually brushing it. Stretch your free leg in front of your skating foot and hold it there for a moment. Now, transfer your weight to the other side. Straighten your right knee and bring your left foot back opposite the right. Bend both knees, keep your body in a neutral position, and again shift your weight to gain the new edge.

Keep practicing this with repetition. Once you are at ease, you might vary the positions a bit, but remember all stroking requires a neutral position of the body when you transfer weight from one side to the other.

## Stopping

It isn't obvious looking at them, but your skates have brakes, too. They are the edges of your skate blades, which can be used to create drag and friction, bringing your gliding to a stop. You must try to scrape or shave the surface of the ice with your blades when you want to stop.

**The T-Stop:** You come to a stop by putting your free foot behind your gliding foot so that it gently scrapes the ice sideways but flatly against your forward glide. You form a T with your feet. Arms are in a forward position. With practice you will learn to control the pressure of your stopping foot for faster or slower stops. Practice the T-stop with both right and left foot. Keep at it until you get it right.

**The Snowplow Stop:** In this stop your blade piles snow up in front of itself as you stop. You bend the knees forward while doing a two-foot glide, then push the feet apart with the toes in and heels out, all the time applying firm pressure on the inside edges to shave the ice. If you vary the angle of your blades, you will find the exact position in which you are most comfortable.

**The Hockey Stop:** The hockey stop is an emergency putting on of the brakes and *must* be learned by every skater. At first try this stop while holding onto the side boards. With your feet pointed ahead, and slightly apart, and with your knees bent, twist your lower body to the left, turning your hips, knees and feet all at the same time. Your shoulders remain square, facing straight ahead. As you turn to the left, keep your feet together, lower your left hip and shoulder and release your weight by rising up on your knees and shifting your weight to the front of the blades. As you stop, return your weight to the balls of your feet and hold your ankles straight.

Of course, you must practice and learn the hockey stop in both directions.

T-Stop Snowplow Hockey stop. Back stop.

Backward swizzle.

# 5 TECHNIQUES OF BACKWARD SKATING

Just as in forward skating, your posture is vital when moving over the ice backwards. Your head must be up, back straight, skating knee bent, arms and shoulders relaxed and your free leg in line. *Do not bend forward from the waist.* And don't push out on one hip and then the other in a backward motion.

When skating backwards your weight must be slightly forward just over the balls of your feet. The blade of your skate (figure or hockey) has a slight curve or rocker which is what allows you to maneuver. While skating backwards your balance point is nearer the front of the blade. Just press down on the balls of your feet.

**Backward Sculling and the Side-to-Side Push:** These are separate methods of skating backwards that often are combined with beginners.

The side-to-side push requires arms and shoulders square, knees bent, weight over both blades, feet fairly close and blades flat on the ice. Turn both heels to one side (the right) by twisting at the waist. When you do this your weight will shift to your right foot on the inside edge, with your free left foot resting lightly on the ice beside it.

This will start your glide to the right and backward. Bend your knees again and with another twist of the waist turn your heels to the left. This will make your weight transfer to your left foot and you will glide backwards to the left. Once some speed is gained bring your feet together in a straight line and glide as far as possible.

To start the backward double scull, your toes must be together and your heels apart so that you are using the inside edges of your skate blades. Bend at the knees and let your feet glide apart. When you reach the width of your shoulders, straighten your knees, come up on the flats of your blades, and draw your feet parallel as you resume a neutral body position.

Repeat this without stopping and add a backward glide with both of your skates close together when you gain speed. Alternate this with the side-to-side push to teach yourself backwards skating.

**Backward Single Sculling:** Now we are going to try and make a nice big capital letter "D" on the ice with your skate blades. With your body in the neutral position place most of your weight on the left foot. Your left ankle must be straight. Turn your right toe in and place that blade on the inside edge. Now, press down on the right foot and make yourself go backwards. As you do this trace a semicircle with your right blade and a straight line with your left. The result is a capital "D."

Reverse the operation with your left foot pushing off and tracing the half circle and your right foot tracing the straight line.

**Backward Stroking:** This seems to happen easily after you have conquered the side-to-side push. After you have some momentum in your glide from either the side-to-side push or single sculling, try to push off with your left foot while transferring all your weight to the right foot. Slowly lift the left foot an inch or two from the ice and keep it in front of you. Press your skating hip downward and maintain your weight over the ball of your skating foot. If it is too far forward your toe pick will catch on the ice and you will fall. If it is too far back, you might catch your heel. Now, bring your feet together and from the neutral position, push off the right inside edge onto your left foot.

When you have mastered this, try it from a rest position. The push off is similar to that in the side-to-side method. Swing your left heel out on its inside edge as in a single scull. Then straighten your left knee and push down on the ice, switching your weight to the right foot and gliding backwards on your right outside edge. Practice starting with each foot and maintain a good body lean, while keeping your feet close together at push off.

**Backward Stopping:** If you have figure skates, the easiest way to stop is to use your toe picks. A one-foot toe scratch is accomplished by gliding backwards on both feet. Slide one blade behind you and raise your heel enough so that the toepick scrapes the ice, slows you down, and finally brings you to a stop.

A two-foot toe scratch is harder, but has more braking power. Again begin gliding backwards, feet parallel, arms outstretched for balance, body straight. Lift both heels at once and allow your toepicks to stop you. You should lean well forward at the stop, but you can regain your speed gradually.

There is also the backward snowplow, in which you glide backward on both feet, knees bent, turn one or both toes out, so that the inside edges shave the ice and bring you to a stop, straightening your knees.

The toughest technique to learn is the Backward T-Stop. Keep your body square, and as you glide backward, place one foot behind you at a right angle; bend your skating knee and lean forward. Stretch the free foot backwards and place it lightly on the ice on an inside edge. Keeping your body square you will learn how to adjust the pressure on the stopping blade, in order not to bring you to a jarring totally sudden stop.

**Backward Outside Edges:** Inside edges are the easiest to learn in forward skating, but when skating backwards this is reversed. You must be comfortable skating backwards before you attempt to learn the back outside edges.

From a neutral position and knees bent, sway your body and arms slightly to the left, standing for an instant or so on your left foot. Now, push off from the inside edge of the left blade, switching your weight to your right foot as you make a backwards circle on the ice in a counterclockwise direction. Keep your right knee bent, and rotate your shoulders to the right, so that your right shoulder and arm are in front. Press your skating hip back hard, and hold your free left foot in front of you over the tracing you are making, toe pointed down. Your whole body leans to the right towards the center of the circle you are making in the ice.

Now gradually transfer your weight from the left thrusting foot to the right skating foot. The thrusting foot travels a short distance until the striking foot takes the ice, and even when this happens the shift in weight should be just starting. Both feet remain on the ice for a short time, but only until the thrust and weight transfer is completed.

To thrust onto a left back outside edge simply reverse the procedure. It is worth repeating that you should learn to skate both ways and not just in the counterclockwise direction most rinks allow public skating.

**Consecutive Backward Outside Edges:** These are best done as swing rolls, with your right back outside edge controlling your movements. Slowly move your free left foot back passing it close to your skating foot, until it is past your line of travel. While your left foot is moving back, rotate your hips and shoulders until your body is square again. Now, bring your skates together, and from the neutral position, strike with your left back outside edge. The push should be from the inside edge of the right blade. It's tougher when you are already moving, but the idea is much the same. Be sure to turn the heel of your thrusting foot out all the way and make your strike with your feet as close as possible.

**Backward Inside Edges:** Backward inside edges are the next step after mastering backward stroking. Skate backwards in a clockwise curve. Pick up your right skate and move it back just inside the tracing. Your right shoulder and hip must be pressed back, as you look back over your right shoulder. Bend your left knee with your body leaning to the right, and your free foot extended in the back. When you lose speed, bring your feet together, and from neutral position. Now try this with your right foot.

To learn backward inside edges from rest, stand with your back to the long axis, feet apart about shoulder width. Rock onto your left skate, then bring the right skate next to it and make a semicircular thrust, with the left foot turning your body so your arms swing to the left. Bend your right knee and keep your left arm slightly forward during the strike. You must lean your body to the left as your right foot strikes the inside back edge. Your left shoulder should be pressed forward and your left skate should be in front as you glide backwards. A lot of practice is usually required—and you must practice this on each foot.

Consecutive back inside edges are almost always problems—and are rarely done as swing rolls.

**Backward Crossovers:** Some skaters claim backward crossovers are easier to learn than forward crossovers, if you have become comfortable skating backwards. They are easier to do in both directions—being employed to

Doing a backward crossover.

go around corners, skate in circles, and create speed when skating backwards.

When skating counterclockwise you should cross the left foot in front of the right foot—switching your weight from your right back outside edge to your left back inside edge.

Begin skating backwards in a counterclockwise direction by holding your right shoulder and arm back in a tightly held checked position. Your head should face the center of the circle you are tracing in the ice.

Bend both knees and press your right hip forward keeping your weight over your skating foot. Lean your body to the right on your right outside edge.

Now comes a sculling thrust with your left foot, but leave it on the ice. While still on the ice, but not holding up any weight, move the left foot across in front of your skating foot.

# 6 RECREATIONAL SKATING

The glamorous gold medal stars who flash across your television screen are not truly representative of the average youngster or oldster who gets some of his kicks from sliding over frozen water. The United States Figure Skating Association understands this, and most rinks would go out of business without recreational skating and hockey skating to pay the bills.

## The Ice Skating Institute of America

Most of the fifty million Americans who skated in 1983 skate for fun, and many of them belong to the Ice Skating Institute of America (ISIA), which has nationwide programs and services for ice skaters of all age levels and skill.

For the very young skater there is the Pre-Alpha Skating Test Program which introduces the young or cautious to skating.

With increasing skill you will perhaps want to try and prove you belong in the world of ice skating by passing the ISIA Alpha, Beta, and Gamma patch tests.

To pass the Alpha test, four basic requirements are tested. They are your forward stroking; forward crossover, right foot over left; forward crossover, left foot over right; and a one-foot snowplow stop.

Beta is the backwards test. Backwards stroking, backwards crossover, left foot over right, backward crossover, right foot over left, and finally a T-stop, right-foot outer edge and a T-stop, left-foot outer edge.

By the time you reach Gamma testing possibilities, you will be far out of the novice class.

On more advanced levels the ISIA has free-style skating tests, with ten separate examinations. By providing direction through a system of graduated objectives, these popular recreational tests effectively develop more advanced skills. Most young skaters really look forward to being awarded their ISIA patches or badges. There is a saying that the world's most difficult free-style test is ISIA Number Ten.

The ISIA also has tests for figure skating, couple skating, shadow skating, and pair skating, also known as partner skating. These tests are very popular nationally. Young skaters who like skating with a partner should consider this route as opposed to the more expensive USFA tests, which are a bit more complicated. Many Ice Skating Institute of America adherents claim the ISIA is the farm team for the United States Figure Skating Association (USFSA).

The ISIA awards handsomely embroidered badges to all ice skaters who pass ISIA examinations. Young skaters are usually very proud of these awards and have them sewn onto their skating clothes. The various different skating specialties each offer different colored badges.

# 7 HOCKEY SKATING

Skating is the most important skill in hockey. If you cannot skate, you cannot play—it's that simple. Skating must be almost as automatic as walking in order to play at any decent level of competitive ice hockey.

We have covered the basic maneuvers of skating in earlier chapters. Hockey skating is essentially founded on these fundamentals, but comments are useful for reinforcement and review of what special knowledge it takes to be a hockey skater—although we cannot cover the rules for playing hockey in this book.*

It is vital to learn to stop, or turn in either direction. Usually when you start, your first few strides are short running steps designed to pick up speed. To start, the skater leans forward and more or less throws himself in the direction he wishes to go. In stopping, the player must simply put most of his weight on the outside of his foot and turn the blades of his skates parallel.

It is important that you learn to skate in both directions by skating both clockwise and counterclockwise. At most rinks three quarters of skating time is clockwise, and it takes an effort to learn the reverse.

Stops and starts help both skating skill and conditioning. A good skating drill is to circle the entire rink in a huge figure eight while circling both nets. Always "cross over" when turning, do not glide around turns. Most young players find it easier to cross the right foot over the left but have difficulty in crossing the left over the right.

Carry the hockey stick when you skate unless forbidden to do so by the rink you are practicing on. It is important to coordinate the movement of your stick with your body as you skate.

---

***Editor's note:** If you want to learn how to play hockey read *Hockey Basics* by Norman MacLean, published by Prentice-Hall, Inc., 1983. Parts of this chapter on skating and power skating have been excerpted from this book.

Also, check your blades before play or practice—they may need sharpening. This will give you a better edge. Sharpening is a must before a game.

**Skating Speed:** In order to fly up the ice, you simply push with one foot and glide with the other. Skating rhythm is everything. The proper coordination of all parts of the body—feet, hips, knees, and shoulders—produces that fluid overdrive, or glide, that is pleasurable. After you get it right, it will seem easy.

Remember when gliding to keep your upper body ahead of your hips. This will help your balance. You must master rhythm or you will forever use choppy strides. The length of your stride is determined by you and what feels best for you.

**Stopping:** When the play reverses and goes in the opposite direction in an instant, everyone on the ice must stop, turn, and go in the other direction in order not to be "trapped" out of the play. Since most hockey stops are made to change direction, bend one knee forward a bit as you stop, and then start the push-off motion needed for a quick start.

**Turning:** In hockey, turns are usually much sharper in their angle than glides and must be made at fairly high speeds. As a result, when turning you must "cross over" on each alternate stride. When turning left, you will cross the right foot over in front of the left and "lean" and "push off" in the direction of the turn. The reverse is true when turning right. The more forcefully you push off after crossing over, the faster you will start in the reverse direction—and perhaps the quicker you will get to the puck.

**Skating Backwards:** Everyone, not just defensemen, must be able to skate backward. You do exactly the same thing you do when skating forward except that you "sit down" in your pants and lean your backside in the backward direction you are skating.

Here are two drills.

*1. Skate backward the entire length of the rink, lifting first one skate and then the other completely off the ice.*

*2. Skating backward, stop at every line, turning left at the first line and right at the next.*

Straight backward start

When skating backward you should "hang" your chest forward in order to maintain balance. Always lift your skates from the ice and push off, don't glide.

## Power-Skating

Power-skating is a term for using the edges of your skate blades, basing all of your movements on the principle of inside and outside edging. Along with this simple concept is the idea of a basic stance, with the knees bent slightly more than the average hockey player is used to, but if perfected will give almost perfect balance on skates.

Each skate blade (defensemen, forwards, and goalies all use slightly different skates) has a hollow running its entire length. The inside of this hollow is called the inner edge, and the outside is called the outer edge.

**The Long Exercise:** Always get into a good hockey position to start power drills. Now push off with either skate to the side, keeping your weight on the ball of the foot. Extend the leg to the fullest, with the skate as close to the ice as possible at the end of the thrust. Then bring the leg back to its original position by executing a letter *C* backward. Bring the foot forward and glide for a count of two. The feet should be a shoulder width apart during the glide.

**The Stride:** The stride is the same as the long exercise, except that you don't glide for the count of two but push off again immediately, guaranteeing more speed. Thrust to the side, with your weight evenly balanced, knees bent, upper body stationary, and head up. Remember that it is not possible to begin the thrust unless both feet are on the ice at the start.

Therefore, when a thrust is completed, make sure your weight is returned completely to the returned foot before beginning the next thrust.

Forward stride sequence and release

The days when a coach simply threw the puck on the ice and let everyone scrimmage while learning to skate on their own are over. In order to play hockey you must spend lots of time skating with guidance.

**Skates**
They are the most important equipment you will own. They come in three different types for hockey. The shoe part should be of strong leather, fit perfectly, and have a strong arch support, or counter, of reinforced material. Buy them from a store specializing in skates.

Forward's skate. Defenseman's skate. Goalie's skate.

## How to Join a Hockey Team

The Amateur Hockey Association of the United States (AHAUS) has 11,000 teams registered in what might be the most organized amateur sport in the United States. That means there are approximately 165,000 players. In addition, those players are served by 8,000 coaches and 8,000 referees.

To join a team go to your nearest skating rink. Almost all rinks run "house" leagues that have AHAUS programs for your age.

Once you get on a team you will receive coaching through AHAUS clinics and the Coaching Achievement Program. An early start in skating helps a player to make the team. After that, playing the game of ice hockey is fun.

AP/Wide World

Elaine Zayak, American figure skater, competing at the 1984 Olympics in Sarajevo.

# 8 FIGURE SKATING

Figure skating is the Cadillac of the world of whiz and whirl—the gold medal glamour part of the sport. Roughly speaking it is divided into compulsory figures, free skating, pair dancing, and ice dancing.

The United States Figure Skating Association (USFSA) is the governing body in the U.S. It conducts tests at the various levels, sponsors competitions, and publishes *Skating Magazine.*

The USFSA has member clubs in almost every locale in the U.S. If you want to become a figure skater, you should join the local club—and enroll in the USFSA.

## Compulsory Figures

Figure skating got its name because at one time early skaters tried to trace actual numbers on the ice. A copy of the USFSA Rule Book will explain this in detail.

In competitions the figures to be skated are selected by drawing lots, with all contestants skating the same figures. At the present time figures count for thirty percent in most events—but in the past they were as much as twice that. Free skating, in which a skater meshes various jumps, spins, and graceful movement with a selected musical piece, now receives a far larger percentage of a competition than in the past. TV emphasizes free skating, despite the fact that compulsory figures at one time were much more important.

Compulsories must be skated on new ice, with judges often getting down on the ice to examine the figures. At your home ice rink you will find that renting a patch of ice, a strip of clean ice about twenty feet wide and about half the length of the rink very early in the morning before school, is the accepted norm for the about-to-be-serious skater.

Figures are really circles. Each figure is skated three times on each foot. During practice a skater might consider using a metal compass called a scribe to measure circles. The scribe draws perfect circles over the natural ones skated by the skater, showing where the skater has made errors. The USFSA has a basic skills test for new skaters. As mentioned previously, the ISIA has its quite famous Alpha, Beta, and Gamma tests for the student of figure skating. The Canadian Figure Skating Association also has a test structure which is fairly close to that used by the United States Figure Skating Association.

The USFSA's test program has a preliminary test and eight figure tests. Before a figure skater can compete in the senior events leading to Olympic competition he or she must pass all eight figure tests, plus the Senior Free Skating tests. Most fall by the wayside.

Before you try serious work on compulsory figures you should learn the following basic skating movements. They are the three turns, the Mohawks, and changes of edge.

**Three Turns:** In the main, they are turns on one foot from an outside to an inside edge, or the reverse, and they can start from either forward or backward skating. In every case the rotation is in the direction of the natural curve you are skating.

THREE TURNS

The right forward outside three is started on an RFO edge with your turn in a clockwise direction. The resultant tracing resembles the numeral three.

The three turns are named for the edge you begin on. While skating on an RFO edge, rotate your shoulders until the left arm and shoulder are in front. Your free left leg is behind with the foot pointing down over your tracing. Now rotate your head and shoulders and hips to the right, while bringing your free foot up behind your right foot. As you do this, straighten your skating knee. This twisting of your upper body, combined with the release of the weight over the blade from raising your right knee, will turn the skate around.

When the skate turns around, sometimes the beginner starts to lose control. As soon as your foot turns, your left arm and shoulder must be pressed back—with the free foot pointing down and over the tracing in front of you. Your head must always face in the direction you are skating. This stops your rotation to the right and enables you to hold your new back inside edge.

**Mohawks:** Mohawks are used in free skating and ice dancing and some of the movement is used in figures. They are turns from a forward edge to a backward edge of the same type. The simplest is the forward inside open Mohawk. It should be done in both directions but most new skaters start on a right forward inside (RFI) edge, in a neutral position with a bent skating knee. When your edge is solid, rotate counterclockwise with your right shoulder leading. Continue rotating your body until both shoulders and head face the tracing, and bring the heel of your free left foot next to the instep of your skating foot at a right angle, something like a T-position. Now place your left foot on the ice on an inside edge with the weight on the ball of the foot. Now gently but firmly press back the right side of your body to check your turn, and extend your right foot over the tracing. The back edge for the Mohawk is the same as the three turn. This is an open Mohawk because the new free foot goes back after the turn. Closed Mohawks are for advanced skaters.

**Changes of Edge:** Changes of edge are moves taking you from one edge to another on the same foot, while tracing an "S" on the ice. They can be done from an outside to an inside edge or vice versa, while skating either forward or backward, and do not involve a turn.

To go from a right forward outside (RFO) to an RFI, begin a swing roll with the right shoulder and hip forward, the left leg and hip pressed down in back. Now, slowly allow the free left foot to come forward and the shoulders and hips to rotate to neutral position. When you approach the axis where you will change the edge, press your free left shoulder back, keeping your shoulders and hips level. At the axis, slightly straighten your skating knee, and bring your free leg back rapidly, at the same time rocking over to the inside edge and bending your right knee as your body goes into neutral position. When you begin skating on the new inside edge your shoulders and hips will be square to the tracing, and your free left leg will be just inside the circle.

As with the three turns and the Mohawks, all changes of edges are made possible because of the release of weight on your skating foot, when your knee flexes, as well as the changing of body position at the same time.

**A Figure Eight:** All compulsory figures are really based on the figure eight. An eight may be started either forward or backwards, and on either an inside or outside edge.

A basic figure eight is made of two circles that run tangent to one another. One circle is skated on each foot. Then these circles are repeated two more times.

The figures you must learn to pass the USFSA Preliminary Test are the forward outside and inside circle eight and the waltz eight.

**Forward Outside Circle Eight:** Stand in the T-position with your back to the middle of the circle you are about to trace. Your shoulders and hips are lined up along the short axis, shoulders level. Keep your head up and look at the ice by moving your eyes, not your head. Push off with the entire side of your blade, not the toe. When you push off, you should leave your left skate behind you in a straight line. Your free left foot is turned down and out, the heel over your tracing. Bend your left knee slightly. As you skate you lean towards the center of your circle with your body moving as one, leaning in one line, and with no hips or shoulders sticking out. Ride the edge, don't try to steer the skate. If your body position is right—and you have aimed the edge correctly at the start—you will make a circle.

Keep this position until you have reached one third of your circle, or if possible, one half. then bring your left arm and your left leg alongside (but not your left shoulder or hip) and pass them in the front. You must keep your shoulders and hips square to the tracing. The free foot now reaches a position in front of the skating foot with the heel over the tracing you are about to make and the toe pointed down and out.

When you move into the final third of your circle, slowly straighten your free left knee until the leg is fully extended in front, but don't lock the knee. Gradually straighten your skating knee. Shoulders and hips must remain square. If everything has been done correctly, you can glide through the last third of your circle.

When you are nearing the center, perhaps two feet away, bring your free foot alongside and take a position with your left arm and hand leading. Bend your knees and push off into the left outside circle.

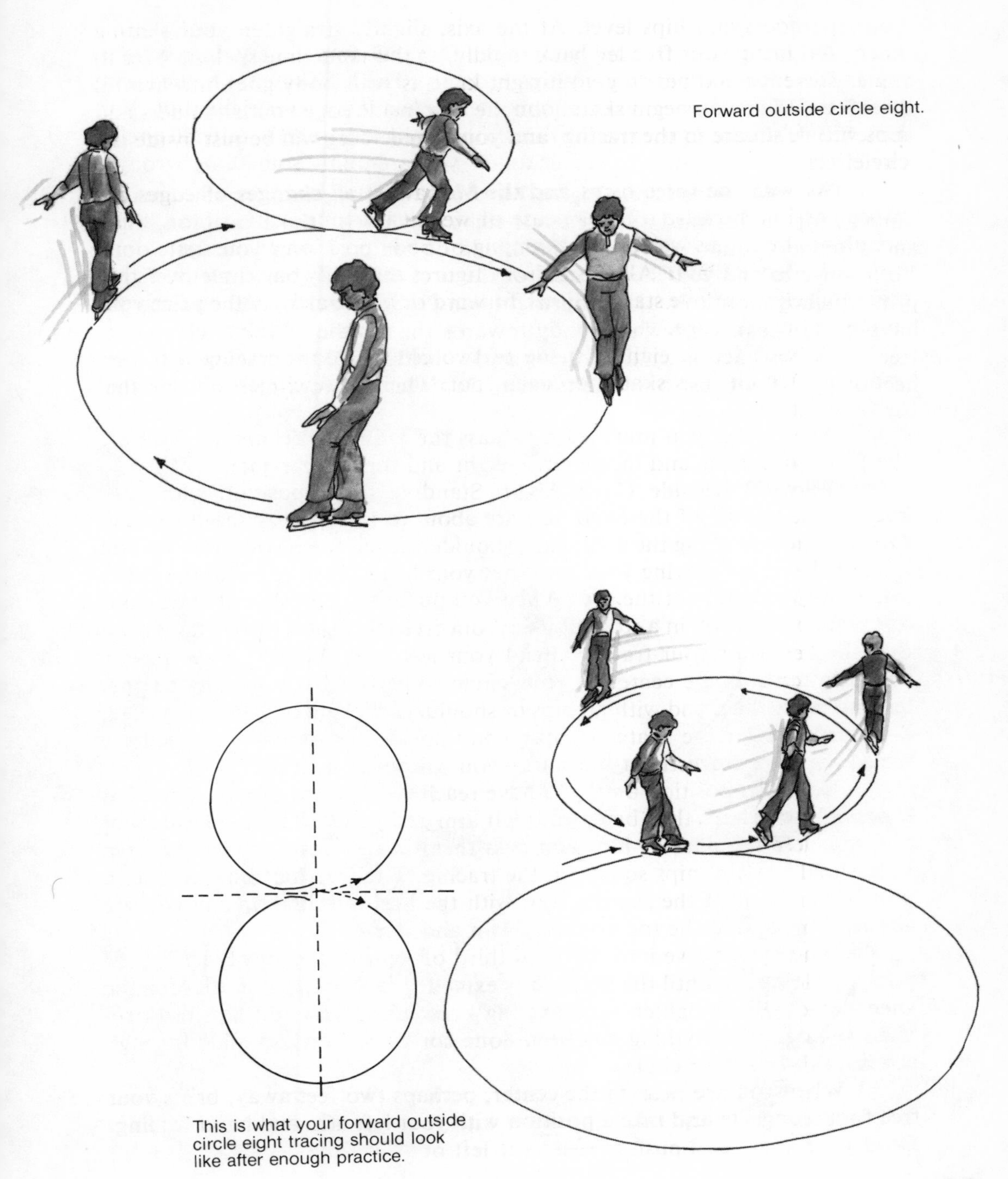
Forward outside circle eight.

This is what your forward outside circle eight tracing should look like after enough practice.

As you push off, turn your right foot out to a ninety-degree right angle. This makes you turn your hips properly. The left skate takes the ice at the center so the curve it makes joins the one made by your right foot. For the left outside circle, reverse the directions given for the right outside circle. The circles should return to center unless you are doing something wrong.

**Forward Inside Circle Eight:** Most of the instructions for this are the same as for the forward outside circle eight. Begin with the T-position, hips and shoulders square. Your weight should be centered over your left foot. Your left arm and your head leads for the first third of your circle over the print you are about to make. Your right hand is held back over the print you have made. Lean your whole body towards the middle of the circle. Your free foot goes back after the tracing and is held inside the tracing with the heel of your boot just over the tracing. Don't let this foot drift outside the

Forward inside circle eight.

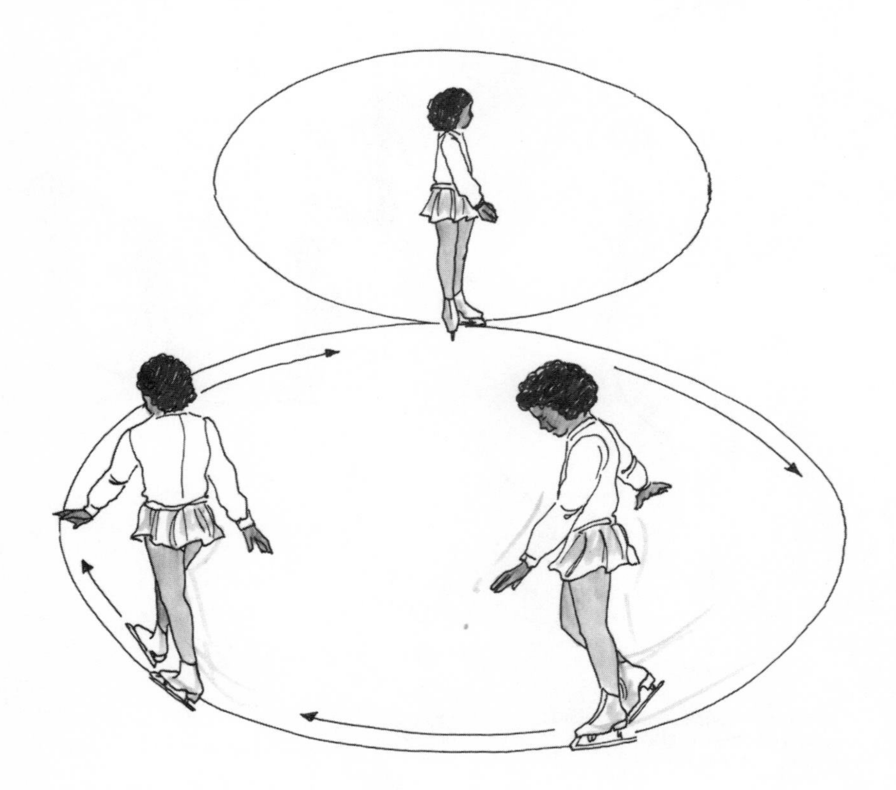

circle. If you do this your tracing will curve inward.

During this part of the circle your hips and shoulders must be square. Be sure your hips are held forward and your weight is balanced just back of the center of your skating blade. This creates a downward pull on your whole spine. You hold your edge by pressing your skating hip in. At the one-third point bring your right arm forward and your left arm back, passing them close to the body. Then, pass your free left foot forward—again keeping your shoulders and hips square to the line of travel. As before, slowly straighten your skating knee as your free foot moves forward. Keep this position until you bring your skates together for the new push off.

Be sure you close your circle and at the center look down and check this. Watch how your circles are lining up and make whatever changes are needed. Practice constantly until you master this.

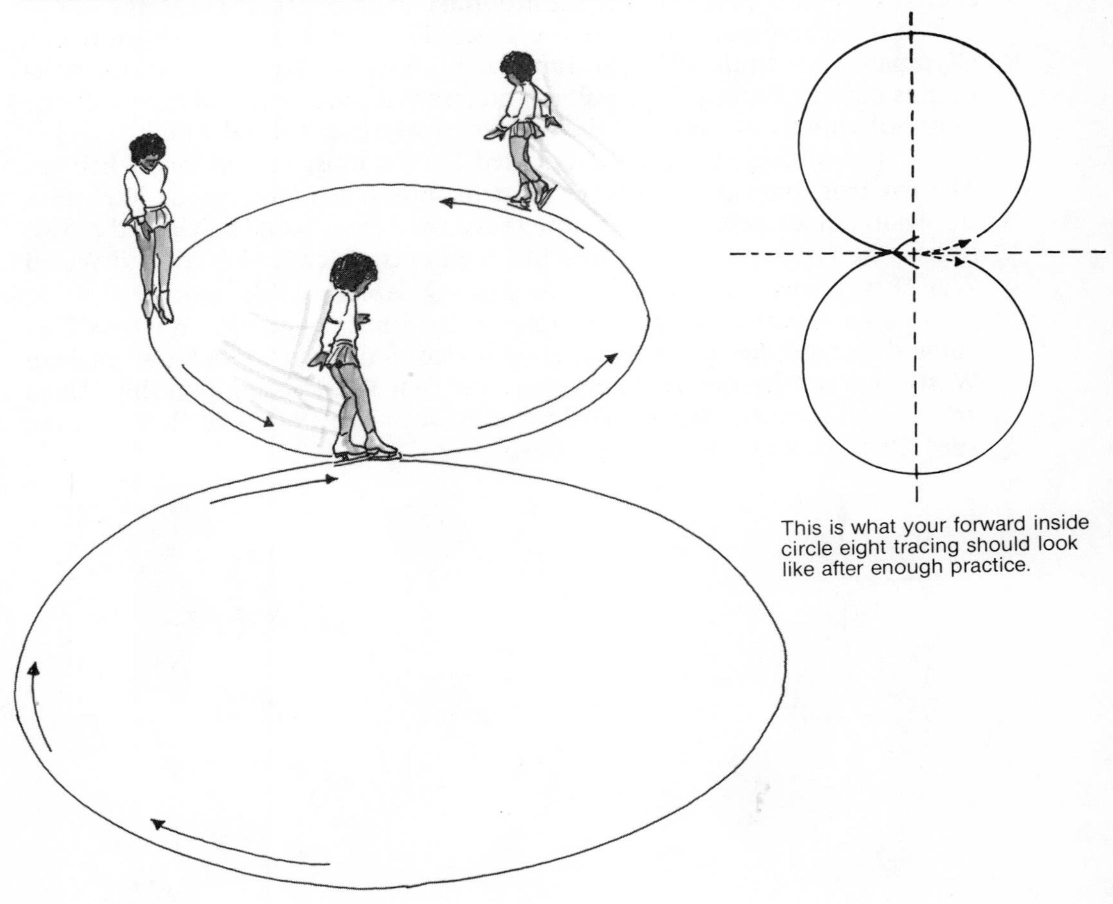

This is what your forward inside circle eight tracing should look like after enough practice.

**The Waltz Eight:** The waltz eight has three sections to each circle. They are a three turn, a back outside edge and a foward outside edge. You must change feet twice in each circle. Each section should cover one-third of the circle.

**Advanced Figures:** Beyond the Preliminary Test are more difficult figures. The entire USFSA test structure is arranged so that a skater must master the simpler figures before moving on to the more complex ones. Many variations are possible. If you want to become a serious skater, infinite time and practice is required. However far you progress—good luck!

## Ice Dancing

Ice dancing has been the fastest-growing aspect of figure skating in recent years and is probably the most popular form of figure skating.

It became part of the World championships in 1952—but wasn't an Olympic event until 1976, at Innsbruck, Austria. Ice dancing traces its origins back to Europe. The waltz or an international march were usually the music of choice, as they lent themselves to whirling around a rink.

The music used today originated for the most part in Great Britain. The fox-trot, paso doble, rocker fox-trot, blues, Viennese waltz, Westminster waltz, quickstep, the Argentine tango, and rhumba all originated at two rinks—the Stretham Ice Rink and the Westminster Ice Rink. Up until World War II these two rinks were the ice dancing capitals of the world.

In a sense the sun has never set on British ice dancing, with Jane Torvill and Christopher Dean carrying on a tradition begun in 1952, when Jean Westwood and Lawrence Demmy won the first World Championship. Dean and Torvill have reigned as World champions since 1981, and they won the 1984 Olympic gold medal at Sarajevo.

Ice dancing has changed dramatically over the years, with the early preference being for very erect posture and very little emphasis being placed on the straight free leg. Now free legs are used in many ways and the bodies flow over the ice at much greater sped. The emphasis, once very strict, has swung from technical excellence to the dancer's artistic presentation. It is not the province of this book to cover ice dancing in any depth, because it is a more advanced aspect of skating. However, the first dances learned are called Compulsory Dances and are used in competitions and tests. In ice dancing, of course, the vital aspect of the whole sport is skating with the music. The right combination of young male and young female can result in the most lovely partnership for beauty, grace, and complete enjoyment on ice.

You will learn to dance to the Mohawks, three turns, and swing rolls you have already learned. The major basic dance steps to master are the chasse, progressives, swing rolls, and forward cross rolls.

The first compulsory dances are the Canasta Tango and the Dutch Waltz. From mastery of these two—there is no limit to what can be accomplished.

## Free Skating

Free skating is the most glamorous aspect of figure skating—the one seen the most on TV. Pivots, spins, spirals, and other jumps can be learned with practice. More advanced jumps require special coaching.

Descriptions of more advanced jumps such as the split, lutz, and axel, are included to indicate what you will need to learn if you are to become a top-notch skater. The USFSA Preliminary Test requires a waltz jump, a salchow, a toe loop, a half lutz, a one-foot spin, and a two-foot spin.

**Spirals:** These resemble a ballet dancer's arabesques. A spiral is a long gliding edge held for a long time until it traces a circular pattern, while the circle becomes smaller and smaller. In spiral position the trunk is horizontal, with the back strongly arched. The free skate is extended straight behind the body with the foot usually at the same height as the head (that's right). The head and shoulders are up, with the hands extended at shoulder level. Spirals can be skated forward or backward, on either foot, on each edge, and with many different arm positions.

**Spread Eagles:** This is done with your hips pressed back and your feet pointing in opposite directions while holding the same edge, either inside or outside. It can be skated clockwise or counterclockwise. A spread can also be skated in a straight line. Feet must be turned out to do a spread eagle and this might require warming up on dry land.

Start at the barrier. With your feet near the boards and your hands on the rail, bring your feet as close together as you can, with heels in and toes

A pivot.

Spread eagle.

out, so that they are almost parallel to the boards. Bend your knees and turn your ankles until you are on the outside edges of your blades. Straighten your knees and tuck in your hips, but drop your ankles. Push along the barrier while holding the outside edges and keeping your knees straight.

**Pivots:** In a pivot a toepick is dug into the ice, as you make small circles around it with your other blade.

A forward inside pivot isn't that hard. Start as if doing an inside Mohawk. When you make your curve smaller, stretch your free foot inside the circle, with your free arm back and the skating arm forward. Drag your pick, put weight on it in the ice, bend your knee over it, and let the other skate pivot in a circle around it. You must always let the pick hold take slowly and form a smaller and smaller circle.

**Spins:** Balance is the key to skating, and practice is the key to spins. You may even feel somewhat dizzy if you spin enough, but you will get used to this. Most coaches recommend that you only spin in your natural direction. The easiest spin to learn is the two-foot spin. This is done on your skate blades, not on the pick. Begin with both skates on the ice 12 inches apart. If

The spin.

you are to spin to the left, first throw your arm and shoulders to the right, then swing to the left, and follow through with your back arm to propel your body into a left spin.

A one-foot spin may be done by picking up one foot during a two-foot spin, but a good one must begin with an approach that builds up speed and rotation.

**Sit Spins:** A sit spin is also called a Jackson Haines, after the man who invented and perfected it. You might try practicing a sit spin in a chair. Your upper body must lean forward in a straight line. Your free foot should be straight in front of you, its heel level with your seat. Hold the boot of the free foot in both hands as you press down on your free knee with the elbow on the same side to keep your toe turned out.

**Jumping:** Position is everything in all jumps. Your knee is a coiled spring which releases your body for your jump. It has to be bent just right to supply this energy. Jumps are easier when done with speed. Speed helps the height and distance of your jump. In addition, all jumps need rotation of the skater's body in the air. This ranges from a half revolution for a waltz jump to three complete revolutions for triple jumps. The rotating force is provided by the action of the arms and free leg as the skater jumps. While in the air, the arms are brought closer to the body to make rotation faster.

Double toe loop.

The basic jumps are the bunny hop, the three jump, and waltz jump, flips, toe jumps, ballet jump, stag jump, and the more advanced toe loop, plus many others.

**The Salchow:** This jump is named after the great Swedish skater, Ulrich Salchow. It is a jump from a back inside edge to a back outside edge on the opposite foot. It is a relatively easy, single-revolution jump. And it can also be a fairly easy double-revolution jump.

Rotation is easy, but gaining height on the jump is not that easy. This is done by application of the right pressure at the right point on take-off—and by having a good check position prepared for the landing. The most common approaches are from an inside Mohawk, or a forward inside three turn.

**The Lutz:** This is similar to the flip, except that it begins from a back outside edge. Because the blade at this point is tracing a curve in a direction

The Lutz.

opposite to the rotation of the jump itself, you must first place yourself to go one way, and then move in the opposite direction. You land on the back outside edge of the other foot.

The Axel.

**The Axel:** This jump is named after its inventor, Alex Paulsen of Norway. It is a one-and-a-half revolution jump from a forward outside edge to a back outside edge on the opposite foot. It is a combination of the waltz jump and the single-loop jump. You start in the position of the waltz jump, and turn backward into a loop-jump position while in mid-air.

**Free-Skating Competitions:** If you have learned to jump well, and can mesh this skill with your earlier ones, you may be ready to enter free-skating competition. This is the really exciting part of figure skating—the thing most top skaters strive for. There are competitions in figures, free skating, pairs, and dancing, and the ultimate goal is advancement to the Nationals competitions yearly, and the Olympics every four years. You will require coaching and many long hours of tedious work, if you make the decision to try and conquer this final challenge in skating. Good Luck!

**Your Own Personal Skating Program:** This is developed around a piece of music—and the selection of the right music is the most important part of developing your program. It needs highlights which are compatible with the type of skating you do, while expressing artistic interpretation.

**Pairs:** This is tough, both physically and mentally, because the selection of the right partner, and the ability to work with that person is so vital to its success. It is free skating at a high level performed by two skaters in unison, to music of their selection, with all the elements of free skating and certain pair moves always included.

Bill Lanigan, former U.S. Olympic star.

# 9 SPEED SKATING

There are just two 400-meter, Olympic-size, speed-skating tracks in the United States, with the main training center being at West Allis, Wisconsin. The other Olympic-size rink is at Lake Placid, New York, the scene of Eric Heiden's unprecedented five-gold-medal sweep in the 1980 winter games.

At the present time, men skate 500 and 1,000 meter sprints, and 1,500, 5,000, and 10,000 meter races; women skate 500, and 1,000 meter sprints and 1,500, and 3,000 meter races.

**Basic Speed Skating Technique:** Do not try to learn to skate with speed skates. Their very length adds to the new skater's problems—the long, flat blades being hard to handle. In addition, speed should not be the name of the game for the novice skater.

Speed skating is completely different from any of the other types of skating. Mostly it is powerful outside stroking and fast counterclockwise turning to the left. Stops, backward skating, and fancy maneuvers are not part of the scene. Getting used to those very long blades will take some time and perhaps a few falls. If you can join your local speed skating club this is a good idea.

Lessons given at the speed-skating club will be the best way to learn speed skating. You must skate in a crouched position with arms held in back, while holding the left wrist with the right hand, or vice-versa. In order to learn the powerful, energy-saving long glide of the speed skater, you must push off with the entire skate blade. Practice counterclockwise crossovers, leaning to the inside and pushing directly to the outside of the circle with both blades. At first you should concentrate on body position and control. Speed will take care of itself later.

**Speed Skating Meets:** When you feel comfortable and are enjoying your speed skates, you may decide to try racing. To become any sort of racer you will need professional instruction. Power, conditioning, and physical shape and technique will determine if you have any future as an active racer.

Technique is a factor in which most of the top-flight Europeans are ahead of U.S. skaters. Proper coordination of arm and leg movements is vital. The position of the body, how the head is tilted, proper stroking, the swing of the arms, the correct method of making turns—all are vital in creating those record times.

# 10 YOUR FUTURE IN ICE SKATING

As we have mentioned, most everyone who skates just skates for fun and reaches a level of ability that makes skating a fun thing, an avocation, and nothing else. But, what about the skaters who aren't just happy with whizzing and whirling around the rink on weekends? Where do they go and what can they do to advance in the area they have chosen?

If you are a very good skater in either figures or speed skating, you will want to enter competition. This will force you to put skating first over everything, keep in top physical condition, and dedicate your life to your progress as a skater. It will also mean lessons at a high level of coaching. If you really advance, you may qualify for World and Olympic competitions in which you will not be paid, but the travel for yourself and members of your family will be. That's not bad.

You must, first, however, join one of the national associations and learn what you can about your chosen skating specialty. If it is speed skating, you will want to contact the two associations:

1. The United States International Skating Association
   Beggs Isle, Oconomowoc, Wisconsin 53066
   *care of* Mr. George Howie
2. The Amateur Skating Union of the United States
   4423 West Deming Place
   Chicago, Illinois 60639

The USISA promotes Olympic-style speed skating and sponsors lessons and meets. It publishes a bulletin for members. The Amateur Skating Association of the United States sponsors speed-skating competitions and supports the Speed Skating Hall of Fame at Newburgh, New York. A quarterly publication, *The Racing Blade*, is available to members only.

The mecca for figure skaters is the United States Figure Skating Association (USFSA), 20 First Street, Colorado Springs, Colorado 80906. The USFSA sets figure skating standards and sponsors tests and competitions at every level including World and Olympic and also maintains records of all tests and competitions.

The USFSA publishes *Skating* magazine with everything about figure skating, including equipment, summer schools, results at all levels, competition dates and "how-to" articles. Another good bet is *Canadian Skater* published by the Canadian Figure Skating Association, 333 River Road, Ottawa, Ontario K1L 8B9.

If you play hockey, the better you skate the better are your chances. U.S. amateur competition is under the direction of the Amateur Hockey Association of the United States, 2997 Broadmoor Valley Road, Colorado Springs, Colorado 80906, *care of* Mr. Hal Trumble.

The Amateur Hockey Association of the United States (AHAUS) sponsors clinics from Alaska to Alabama, and coordinates the establishment of leagues from mite to senior. There are eight junior leagues (up to 20) in the U.S. presently, all formed with AHAUS assistance.

Another path to the National Hockey League (NHL), if that is your goal, is through high school, prep school, and collegiate hockey. In the past, Canadian junior hockey was the route to the NHL, but now many players, both American and Canadian, receive their final polishing in U.S. colleges.

However, we still recognize that beginning skaters and those who just skate for fun are ninety-nine percent of all those who venture onto frozen water. Their best bet is The Ice Skating Institute of America, 1000 Skokie Boulevard, Wilmette, Illinois 60091. The Ice Skating Institute of America is tied in with almost all the rink operators in the U.S. It conducts recreational tests (Alpha, Beta, Gamma) in figures, pairs, hockey, dance, and speed skating. Most likely, your local rink is a member and can give you the needed information.

Most girls who are hooked by the world of ice skating aspire to skate in one of the touring ice shows. It is a tiring grind after the first year or so, after the thrill of travel has faded. For each star skater with top billing there are 20 or so in the chorus line who are just scratching out a living.

Finally, if you reach a certain level, you might qualify as a skating professional. You would then teach beginning and intermediate skaters all those things you worked so hard to learn—and get paid for it.

Right now, the real demand for skating pros is in the field of recreational skating. Municipal recreational departments, ice rinks, prep schools, high schools, universities, and colleges offer skating lessons at the beginning level. Also, good hockey players may have to start at the junior level, but there are always openings for coaching positions in high schools, prep schools, and colleges. Good luck in whatever area you aspire to.

Albright, Tenley / 5
Amateur Hockey Association of the
  United States (AHAUS) / 29, 47
Amateur Skating Union of the
  United States / 46
backward skating:
  backward crossovers / 22, 23
  backward inside edges 22
  backward outside edges / 21
  backward sculling and
   side-to-side push / 19
  backward single sculling / 20
  backward stopping / 20
  backward stroking / 20
Beloussova, Ludmila / 5
Broadmoor, Colorado Springs, CO / 6
Button, Dick / 5
Canadian Figure Skating Association / 32, 47
*Canadian Skater* / 47
Carruthers, Peter / 9
clothing / 9
Cousins, Robin / 6
Curry, John / 4, 6
Dean, Christopher / 6, 38
Demmy, Lawrence / 38
Edinburgh Skating Club, Scotland / 5
Fassi, Carlo / 6
figure skating:
  advanced figures / 38
  changes of edge / 33, 34
  compulsory figures / 31, 32
  figure eight / 34
  forward inside circle eight / 36, 37
  forward outside circle eight / 34, 35
  free skating:
   Axel, the / 42, 43
   free skating competitions / 43
   jumping / 41
   Lutz, the / 42
   pairs / 43
   personal skating program / 43
   pivots / 40
   Salchow, the / 42
   sit spins / 41
   spins / 40, 41
   spirals / 39
   spread eagles / 39
Fleming, Peggy / 6
foward skating:
  alternating edges / 17
  edges / 16
  forward crossovers / 15
  forward outside edge / 16
  stroking / 14
Glacarium, first artificial ice rink, the / 5
Haines, Jackson / 5
Hamilton, Scott / 6
Heiss, Carol / 5
Henie, Sonja / 5, 6
hockey skating:
  long exercise, the / 18
  power skating / 28
  skating backwards / 27
  skating speed / 27
  stopping / 27
  stride, the / 28
hockey team, how to join a / 29
ice dancing / 5, 38, 39
ice shows, touring / 47
ice skates:
  double runner / 7
  figure skate / 8
  hockey skate / 8, 29
  single runner / 7
  speed skating skate / 8
ice skates, care of / 10
ice skates, how to buy / 8, 9
ice skates, parts of / 7, 8, 9
ice skating, basic steps of:
  dipping / 12
  fall, how to / 13
  foward swizzle / 12
  get up, how to / 13
  gliding / 12
  one-foot glide / 13
  skating forward (sculling) / 12
  standing / 11
  walking / 11
Ice Skating Institute of
  America (ISIA) / 6, 24, 32, 47
International Skating Union / 6
ISIA test programs and awards / 24-25
Jenkins, David / 5
Jenkins, Hayes Alan / 5
Lanigan, Bill / 44
Lynn, Janet / 6
music of Johann Straus / 5
National Hockey League (NHL) / 47
Netherlands, the / 4
Olympic games / 5
pair skating / 5
Philadelphia Skating Club and
  Humane Society / 5
Pre-Alpha Skating Test Program / 24
Protopopov, Oleg / 5
*Racing Blade, The* / 46
recreational skating / 24-25
Rodnina, Irina / 5
Saint Lidwina / 4
Sarajevo, Yugoslavia / 6, 30
*Skating* / 31, 47
speed skating / 45
Speed Skating Hall of Fame / 46
stopping:
  back stop / 18
  hockey stop / 18, 27
  snowplow / 18
  T-stop / 18
Torvill, Jane / 6, 38
Ulanov, Alexei / 5
United States Figure Skating Association
  (USFSA) / 25, 31, 32, 46
United States International Skating
  Association (USISA) / 46
USFSA test program / 32, 34, 39
Vienna / 5
von Szabo-Planck, Heima / 5
Zaitzev, Aleksandr / 6
Zayak, Elaine / 30